100+ CASE STUDIES

PROPERTY NIGHTMARES

Learn from the mistakes of others to become a smarter investor

Dear Mike

Thanks for being awesome

PROPERTY NIGHTMARES

Angelos Sanders

Angelos.

First Printed, 2021

ISBN 978-1-5272-6301-7

www.propertynightmares.co.uk

For my friend, **Phil Oke**.

You were one of the best and possessed a rare talent much respected by all. Not only that, but your pop music knowledge was also unrivalled.

For my children, **Alexander and Athena,** without whom, this book would have been published a year earlier.

Acknowledgements

The effort involved in writing this book has been Herculean and a massive thank you is owed to the many contributors who have helped share their experiences in this book.

Special recognition is due to the following people for their support, who helped with the peer review and provided invaluable feedback, to make this a better book.

Thea Sanders (long suffering wife whose patience and support makes her a legend in her own lifetime).

Val McKie

Jo Lines

Vicki Wusche

Tina Walsh

Andrew Rowell

Contributors

These amazing people helped make this book what it is.

In alphabetical order:

Adrian Wilkes LLB (Hons)

Owner of House2Home Lets Ltd

www.house2homelets.co.uk

A. E. Verona Cocks

Joint Managing Partner and Head of Commercial Dispute Resolution at Paddle & Cocks LLP, Solicitors

www.paddleandcocks.co.uk

Andy Price

Owner and Solicitor

Bright Solicitors

www.brightllp.co.uk

Ashley Smith FCCA CTA ATT

Tax Adviser

www.hmwilliams.co.uk

Barbara Hosker

Entrepreneur, Fulfillionaire & Problem Solver

Dan Anson-Hart

Property developer, investor, PIG Cornwall host and podcaster

www.cornwalllivingproperty.com

Darren Clegg BA (Hons)

Partner specialising in Property Disputes at Paddle & Cocks LLP, Solicitors

darren.clegg@paddleandcocks.co.uk

Dave Ottley

Managing Director

Balance for Business Limited

www.balanceforbusiness.co.uk

Dean Girvan

1st Call Southwest Locksmiths

www.1stcallsouthwestlocksmiths.co.uk

Francis Dolley

Rent 2 Rent Trainer, Author, Speaker and Motivator

www.multiletcashflowsystem.com

Graham Barton

Auctioneer and Chartered Surveyor

As seen on BBC 1 'Homes Under The Hammer'

Ian George

Director

Ocean City Properties Ltd

Jackie Tomes

Founder & CEO Tomes Homes and The Property Strategist

www.tomeshomes.com

www.property-strategy.com

James Barron MRICS

Chartered Building Surveyor

Business Owner

www.barronsurveying.co.uk

James Clarke

Director – Lang Town & Country

www.langtownandcountry.com

Jo Lines

Property Investor and Mentor and Business Consultant

Ambition Property Group & Ambition Growth Network

jo@ambitionpropertygroup.co.uk

Latoya McDonald

Harcourt White Property

Latoya@HarcourtWhite.co.uk

www.HarcourtWhite.co.uk

Lee Gough

Property Investor

www.belgraveproperty.com

Luke Behenna

LMB Insurance services

www.lmbinsurance.co.uk

Mark Homer

Developed/refurbished around 600,000+ sq. ft of buildings and currently manages a residential and commercial property portfolio with a value in excess of £70m+ as an equity holder.

Landlord of 17 years with a personal portfolio valued at £35M+. Co-founder and owner of Progressive Property.

Co-founder and owner of Progressive Lets, a lettings agency which manages around 1,000 tenants and author of five books on Property Investment, Development and Business, one of which is internationally published in three languages.

Michael Foulkes PhD MICE

Chartered Civil Engineer

Mike O'Shea

Director of Kook Interiors LTD

www.kookltd.co.uk

Peter Hill

Mark Holt & Co Chartered Accountants, and Healium LLP business consultants.

Author of 'Pricing for Profit'

www.markholt.co.uk

Phil Oke

Solicitor

Richard Mitchell

Investor

Roy Inman

Investor and entrepreneur

Steve Dorrans

Rent To Rent Veteran

Stuart Hallworth BSc (Hons) MRICS

Chartered Surveyor, Property Investor, Author, Educator and creator of “Surveying Houses with Stuart” course.

stuart@hallworthresidential.com

Sue Pope

Fire Risk Assessor and Health & Safety Consultant

www.firesafetysw.co.uk

Tina Walsh

Author – Property Investor

Sourcing Agent – Sourcing Compliance Expert

Founder and CEO: National Association of Professional Sourcing Agents (NAPSA)

www.getpropertycompliant.co.uk

www.napsa.org.uk

Tishka Chapman

Partner and Licensed Conveyancer at Wolferstans LLP

www.wolferstans.com

Vicki Wusche

Wealth Strategist, Property Investor, Sourcer and Mentor and International speaker

Author of five best-selling books, including Business Awards Finalist: The Wealthy Retirement Plan: A revolutionary guide to living the rest of your life in style. Responsible for client portfolio in excess of £12.5m

Over 11 years' experience as an investor, qualified Master NLP Practitioner and former University lecturer. Now guest on over 80 podcasts internationally.

www.VickiWusche.com

Disclaimer

The boring (but necessary) bit...

Despite the title Property Nightmares, this book is about positivity and learning from other's experiences. This book is written to help inspire and share wisdom to all, in particular for those people who have a passing interest in the world of property, or someone who is already involved in the industry. It is not a name and shame book. The stories that were written by contributors, were sent to the author with no personally identifiable details present, thus preserving anonymity and upholding Data Protection laws. Adding one step further to the abstraction, and diluting similarities to actual persons or events, details within the stories have been changed, but the core message remains. Where names are needed to assist the reader with understanding the story, character names from William Shakespeare's books have been used for characters within the story. Any similarity to actual persons, living or dead, or actual events, is purely coincidental.

The publisher and the author are providing this book and its contents on an "as is" basis and make no representations or warranties of any kind with respect to this book or its contents. In addition, the publisher and the author assume no responsibility for errors, inaccuracies, omissions, or any other inconsistencies herein. Content contained or made available through this book is not intended to and does not constitute legal advice or investment advice or any other type of advice and no relationship is formed whatsoever. The information should never be used without first consulting with a financial or legal professional to determine what may be best for your individual needs. The information provided in this book is for informational purposes only and is not intended to be a source of advice with respect to the material presented. Always seek professional advice before making any kind of investment and you should never make any investment decision without first consulting with your own financial advisor and conducting your own research and due diligence.

The publisher, the author and all contributors do not make any guarantee or other promise as to any results that may be obtained from using the content of this book. To the maximum extent permitted by law, the publisher and the author disclaim any and all liability in the event any information, commentary, analysis, opinions, advice and/or recommendations contained in this book prove to be inaccurate, incomplete, or unreliable, or result in any investment or other losses. No responsibility will be accepted by the publisher or author for materials provided by third parties, including websites.

By reading this book, you agree that you do so at your own risk, are voluntarily participating in these activities, assume all risk of to yourself, and agree to release and discharge the publisher, the author, and all contributors from any and all claims or causes of action, known or unknown, arising out of the contents of this book.

The publisher, the author and all contributors make no guarantees concerning the level of success you may experience by following the advice and strategies contained in this book, and you accept the risk that results will differ for each individual. The stories and examples provided in this book show exceptional results, which may not apply to the average reader, and are not intended to represent or guarantee that you will achieve the same or similar results. The use of this book implies your acceptance of this disclaimer.

Now that's out of the way, we can get on with the book!

Contents

Introduction

Welcome to the world of property!

If you look at the UK's top 100 rich list, most of the people on it have some kind of property as an asset, helping them to increase their net worth. This book is designed to help you look at investing in property the smart way.

Property is often seen as a good investment and it is of no surprise that many people are attracted to investing their hard-earned money in bricks and mortar. Sometimes this can be quite lucrative and the owner experiences very little drama and all is well with the world, but the chances are that most of us have experienced some kind of issue or nightmare and that is what this book explores.

Property Nightmares is different from other property books as it delves into the many and varied experiences of a wide range of people involved in property. It contains stories of the good, the bad and the ugly and it provides a brilliant resource to help you avoid the snags and snares of working in property. It has many inspiring stories showing how to triumph over disaster and it is a way to help you accelerate your success in property. The author and contributors have given their time and considerable experience to help you learn from their mistakes and that is the cornerstone of this book but to also help you answer the below questions.

- Are you tempted by property investing? Could it be a great way of investing or could you find yourself dragged into a nightmare?
- Are you looking to get started in property but are daunted by some of the horror stories you have heard?
- Are you an experienced investor looking to pick up some more tips to add to your success?
- Do you wish to gain knowledge and learn from the experiences of others to avoid making the same costly mistakes and become a smarter investor?

By the end of this book you will either be excited by the challenges you potentially face or so horrified by the stories you have read that you will decide that property investment isn't for you. Either way, you could find that this book is the inspiration that spurred you on to greater things, whatever path you choose. Sometimes knowing what we do not want is just as important as knowing what we do want and by the end of this book your path will be much clearer.

Why I wrote this book

***"Experience is something you don't get until just after you need it."* - Steven Wright**

I wish I had had a resource like this book when I first started out investing in property. It would have saved me so much time and money. People tell me how invaluable the experiences that I have shared have been to them, and knowing how people had benefited from them, became my motivation for collating and curating the experiences of other professionals, as well as my own, to write this book.

The aim is to inspire and support both the existing and the next generation of property people. Within this book, there are certain stories with opposing viewpoints and these have been included intentionally in order to help the reader understand the different viewpoints and form a balanced view on the particular subject.

You are now in possession of a valuable resource that will help you avoid the many common property related mistakes that people make. This will put you on a pathway to navigate the trials and tribulations investors face and help make your property investment journey a more enjoyable and successful one.

This book is a skilful collection of stories with a summary of the key lessons learnt and tips to guide you around the hazards. From buying blind at auctions, to dealing with Iron Man, to collapsing properties, this book has stories that will open your eyes to the potential of any similar issues you might face in the future.

The stories contained in this book are wide-ranging and have been shared by many different contributors. The writing style of the contributors has been preserved as much as possible and that is evident throughout the many stories in this book. This helps illustrate that the world of property is shared by people from all walks of life. You may also notice that some authors straddle multiple sections due to their varied experiences.

You need sheds loads of resilience to survive in the property industry. You face so many potential challenges, some that you will see coming and some that will completely blindside you. Whether it is a property or a people related issue, you need to be prepared for anything.

It is not the scale of adversity that hits you, it is how you overcome it.

Remember, life is full of challenges and it is your job to be as prepared as possible.

Investing in the world of property usually means you have to acquire many skills across many different industries (especially in the beginning; later you can delegate roles to staff or service providers). This book will help you understand the terminology different professionals use and that will allow you to be more effective when communicating with the many and varied professionals you will encounter.

How to use this book

This book can be read in many different ways. Much like everyone's idea of investing in property is different, so too is their preferred way of learning. This book has been written so that you can:

- Read it cover to cover as a straight read,

or

- Use it as a reference guide, as each chapter contains standalone stories that will be relevant to you.

The book has been divided into four different sections to help you navigate it easily.

1. Buying Nightmares
2. Refurb Nightmares
3. People Nightmares
4. Property as a Business Nightmare

The four sections are as follows:

Section One - follows the progress of multiple property purchases and the tales of woe that were experienced.

Section Two - refurbishing a property can be one of the most stressful things that anyone can experience. We all have experienced or know of someone who has experienced a nightmare situation with refurbishing a property.

Section Three - explores the complex and sometimes acrimonious relationship between people and property. We have all heard of nightmare tenants and nightmare landlords but these are just two examples of people nightmares. This section aims to give a balanced view of all parties.

Section Four - dives into the finer details of owning a property related business. If you want to or are running a property business, then the lessons contained here could help increase the standards across the board and gives you greater awareness of how to grow your business and become more efficient.

What this book is not

This book is not about naming or shaming, nor is it written in a way to cause anyone embarrassment. The book was written as a resource to help you navigate and avoid similar mistakes that others have experienced. As mentioned, where names are needed to assist the reader with understanding the story, character names from William

Shakespeare's books have been used as a substitute for characters within the story.

About the Author

James Bond, male model, and International Man of Mystery - these are just some of the terms that have never been used to describe me.

I'll start with a little bit about myself just to put my experiences into perspective. So, please sit back, relax and enjoy!

2007 was the year I started investing in property. Once I realised that there was another way of creating an income rather than relying on the 9-5 job; that was it for me, I had truly caught the investing bug. I have since built a significant portfolio that allows me to work on my passions in life and to help others achieve similar success. By the age of 31, I had left the corporate world behind once and for all and with the companies I had built up, I continued to grow both my property and events businesses full time.

It isn't always easy being an entrepreneur, but the good days outnumber the bad ones and I still get a real kick from transforming a rundown and old property into somewhere people love to live. I also enjoy helping my mentees make their dreams become a reality.

Nobody is perfect and despite our best intentions, we all make mistakes. I am the first to hold my hand up and admit that I am not perfect (despite what my mum tells me) and I have no doubt made mistakes in my time as a property investor, but it is the lessons learnt from those mistakes that make me a better investor and provide a better service for my customers.

Some of the challenges I have faced have been surviving the recession of 2008, a global pandemic and on a local level, changing demands of the student HMO market, including the many nightmares I have written about in this book. Despite these challenges, I have managed to overcome, adapt and thrive.

I have also been featured on the BBC, The Independent, many podcasts and other media about my property experiences and books.

Professional Investment Group aka PIG

When I first started out in property, I realised that it was quite a lonely journey with little support and even fewer people to bounce ideas off. I decided to do something about it. I created the Professional Investment Group, affectionately known as PIG, which is a unique monthly network meeting where like-minded entrepreneurs meet to discuss property, business and listen to experienced and influential guest speakers.

The group started with seven people sat around my living room by the roaring fire and now has thousands of members across the southwest of the UK. PIG has had many local, national, international, and even celebrity speakers present to the delight of the audiences.

The PIG network has enabled many investors go from novice to experienced investor via its great support network and access to great professionals. Get involved by visiting www.pig.network

Your Success Podcast

Never one to stay still for too long, I started a podcast called 'Your Success Podcast' with Mo Haykir, which is a podcast focussing on success, property, and business. I am really proud of the work that has been done with the podcast going from nothing to something that continues to inspire thousands of people regularly across the globe.

I have interviewed many successful people from all walks of life across the world, so if you would like to be inspired and motivated, then have a listen.

Have a listen to the interviews with amazing and inspirational people at www.yoursuccesspodcast.com

Your Success Book

As a result of interviewing and learning from so many successful people on the podcast, it allowed me and my co-author Mo Haykir, to write the Amazon Number 1 Bestselling book, Your Success!

Your Success has sold copies all around the world and has helped inspire many people to become the best version of themselves.

Your Success book dives deep into what makes a successful person successful. Drawing upon our own experiences and that of the interviewees, we distilled the wisdom down to 10 common traits of success that anyone can use to help become the best version of themselves.

Grab yourself or a friend who needs some motivation, a copy at:

www.amazon.co.uk -> Your Success

Mentoring

I really enjoy seeing others become successful as I can understand the journey and challenges involved with becoming a success. I mentor a select few investors who are starting out on their journey to become self-sufficient with income generated from creating a property portfolio. I help motivate and create a plan with them with the goal of creating their own successful portfolio with the ultimate aim of either leaving their job or really taking their investing to the next level. Most importantly, I help keep them accountable and give them access to my power network.

Here are a couple of testimonials from mentees I have helped achieve success:

"Having a mentor such as Angelos has enabled me to fast track my property journey and within 12 months I was financially free. Mentoring with Angelos kept me focused, objective clear and having that accountability really has helped push me forward to where I wanted to

be. Having access to Angelos's experience and contacts was invaluable and offered a huge beneficiary to the mentoring programme. Highly recommend and I know anything is possible with the right guidance." **J. Baker**

"Angelos saved me £20,000 in one afternoon! We did some figures and it would have taken about 24 years (with rent from this one property deal) to make that £20,000 back!" **T. Smith**

I have helped my mentees leave their job and replace their income through property. If this is something you are interested in, then get in touch at www.angelossanders.com

You can also follow my antics below:

Facebook: Angelos Sanders

Instagram: angelossanders

Twitter: @juststartrek

www.angelossanders.com

www.pig.network

www.yoursuccesspodcast.com

www.juststartrek.com

Keep in touch

Please join my mailing list via www.propertynightmares.co.uk to get access to regular updates as well as book and podcast releases.

I would love to know your thoughts on this book and hear about your favourite stories!

Let's go and do this!

PART 1

BUYING NIGHTMARES

Introduction

One of the most significant and most important things that you can ever purchase in your life is a property.

For most of us, it is usually the most expensive thing that we will ever buy. On the surface both the buyer and seller want the same thing and that is for the property to change hands at a fair price. We all hope that the process can be a relatively smooth one, expecting maybe a couple of hiccups along the way. The reality is often quite different and it can end up as a real emotional rollercoaster ride for all involved. It is often said that buying a house can be one of the most stressful events in a person's life.

Buying a property is, as we know, not just simply a transaction between two people. There are usually many other parties included in the process to help complicate matters more.

For example,

- Buyers and/or sellers
- Estate agent
- Letting agent
- Auctioneer
- Mortgage broker
- The solicitor for the buyer
- The solicitor for the seller
- The solicitor for the lender
- The lender
- The lender's surveyor
- A specialist surveyor
- A builder to quote for works
- Planning department
- Building Regulations department
- Land Registry
- Investors
- Insurer

- A gazumper
- A gazunderer

And to top it all, a complete randomer, such as a nosy/envious neighbour or a general busybody, could be determined to get involved – no wonder buying property can sometimes be a nightmare!

When the purchase is in a chain, you potentially have to multiply the above by two or more. Each of these individuals have their own priorities and agendas. Then there is that precious thing called ego, that can sometimes derail a purchase, even with the simplest of transactions. All parties often play out what seems right and fair to them and act out of 'principle', even if it is to their detriment and they ignore the bigger picture. "Principles can be very costly" an estate agent once wisely told me.

Occasionally, a property purchase will sail through in a short amount of time with no dramas and everyone is happy, but that is the subject of another book.

This section on buying nightmares highlights the different problems and nightmares that various people have encountered when buying property. It is filled with stories from brokers, developers, auctioneers and solicitors. It includes planning issues, valuation problems, buying off plan, buying abroad, complex purchases, the importance of surveys and also the very emotional cost of buying property.

The stories in the Buying Nightmares section cover:

- Buying at Auction
- Legals and Finance
- Purchase Surveys
- An assortment of random stories

Chapter 1

Buying at Auction

Modern Auctions

By Adrian Wilkes

A couple of years ago I was travelling in Asia and had decided to bid on a two-bedroom flat which was in a 'modern auction', which for anyone who has come across these things before knows they are probably the most infuriating (and expensive) way to purchase a property – basically the auction deadline gets extended if someone bids in the last five minutes of the auction.

I was eagerly positioned in a space with good mobile reception – my backdrop was the Hong Kong skyline which was suitably lit up and having its nightly laser show. I bid, became the highest bidder, and was quickly replaced by a new 'high bidder' (and the end date of the auction was subsequently extended by a further five minutes); this pattern continued for several minutes, before I was the high bidder and the clock was in its last 60 seconds – I was confident that I had won and went off to enjoy the rest of my evening and celebrated with a few drinks. When I woke up the next day, I found that I had been outbid in the last 30 seconds!

Luckily for me, I knew of another auction that was coming up two days later – there was a property in that auction that I had been attempting to buy for the last six months or so, however, it was a repossession and the solicitors on the other side were anything but speedy. Luckily, since I had been trying to buy it, my solicitor had already been through the legal pack, so that side of things was ticked off, however, I hadn't intended bidding at this auction, and I was on the other side of the world and very much outside of the 'remote bidding' timings. Luckily, I had purchased from them previously and my solicitor was able to verify my identity etc. so I was able to bid and win the auction.

All was well, and I still had a couple weeks left of my holiday. A couple of weeks later, my solicitor got in touch to ask where the completion monies were – I was travelling back that day via Doha and said, I will sort it when I'm back as I had four weeks in which to complete; it was at this point he pointed out that the Special Conditions on the lot meant that there was a 14-day completion period. Not having any of my main account details with me, I spent the 12-hour overnight layover in Doha scrambling around with the account details I did have to hand to pull together the cash for the purchase.

Key lessons learnt:

- Avoid 'modern auctions' – especially given the weighting of the fee structure.
- Don't celebrate too soon and read the small print of auction catalogues.
- If you're going away and likely to purchase something, carry all relevant account details etc. with you.
- By building relationships with solicitors and auctioneers etc. I was still able to get something done whilst being very far away from home – don't underestimate the value of keeping a trusted set of people rather than flitting and changing relationships.

Barn Planning Issue

By Graham Barton

Buying at auction shouldn't result in unfortunate surprises especially if you follow the 'three golden rules':

1. **Viewing the property** - either carrying the requisite construction knowledge yourself or taking someone with you who does.

2. **Reading the legal pack** – this is the conveyancing documentation provided by the selling solicitor.

3. **Having the money ready to complete** – the required 10% auction-day cash deposit is something that you'll probably have fairly readily to hand. However, the moment the auctioneer's gavel falls the clock begins to tick down to the day of completion when the 90% balance is due in cleared funds which is typically only twenty business days later.

However, even behaving responsibly doesn't guarantee safety as the sale of a barn and some land that sold for well over £175,000 is testimony to.

The property, an old farm building, was basically built of concrete blocks and galvanised iron sheets with structural timbers the size of trees, largely because they were actual trees! It was somewhat ramshackle but nevertheless benefitted from what's known as a Class Q approval for residential use.

This is basically a planning consent for conversion to a dwelling of a building that otherwise wouldn't have been considered by the local planners to be worthy of retention. However, Central Government has now directed otherwise and many amazing new homes now stand where eyesores once stood.

The problem is that at a local level, planners had a bit of a grudge about being told to allow new homes in the countryside on the Class Q basis so when a storm hit the barn in question and bits flew off and fell down, they removed the consent on the rather harsh basis that the building was no longer capable of conversion and instead now needed rebuilding which was contrary to the rules of Class Q qualification.

This turn in events coupled with the specific requirements for a new owner to become a successful Class Q applicant meant that as far as I'm aware the barn still stands there as a very, very expensive wreck and a detriment to the countryside, rather than being a wonderful addition to the vicinity and providing a sizeable chunk of Council Tax income for the local council.

Restrictive Covenants for Eighteen Flats

By Graham Barton

Sometimes getting hold of the auction legal pack and having a quick read with relatively civilian eyes can be OK, but not always by any means.

A large house had been awarded planning consent for conversion into eighteen flats and the details of the approval were in the legal pack. This is what the auction buyer focussed on, proceeding to bid despite the fact that the title included a one-hundred-year-old restrictive covenant against sub-division into flats. They thought that if the building had modern-day planning consent that automatically quashed any conflictive covenants.

Well, their solicitor could have told them that wasn't the case, if they had been given sight of the documents before auction day. Instead the solicitor had to tell them after their purchase when they presented the pack to the solicitor as a done deal that they couldn't implement the approved development scheme without being in breach. It was an expensive error because the auction buyer had no choice but to cut a deal with the organisation that benefitted from the covenant and who owned other properties in the area. The outcome was that they were forced to hand over £4,000 per consented flat to lift the restriction which came to a rather painful £72,000.

The House that Fell into the Sea

By Graham Barton

And then there's people who 'buy blind'. Yup, they've not seen the property, not read the auction legal and yet they're still willing to spend thousands of pounds on a wing and a prayer.

I see it time and again from my place on the rostrum and it's nearly always people who've lost out on an earlier lot and who don't want to go home empty-handed. I watch them glance at their catalogue and stick a hand up without a care in the world. Sometimes this method is fine but all too often the lack of knowledge whether it's of the property or the legal pack itself bites back! I've sold a holiday home to a couple who didn't know that the annual fees were more than they'd paid for the actual three bedroomed cabin itself, an attic having planning for a two bedroomed penthouse flat with the bidder thinking he'd got "a right bargain" until he re-read the catalogue entry that evening and realised that the flat hadn't already been created, it was yet to be formed and finally, a five bedroomed detached bungalow on a large plot but with declared subsidence and mining issues that the winning bidder hadn't given themselves time to read about.

In the vast majority of cases, property nightmares at auction are the fault of one person, and it's not the auctioneer!

However, the most graphic example of what not to do at auction was ten years ago when someone bought a property crucially without having viewed it. This was a costly omission from the normal process of due diligence prior to purchase because a site visit would have shown how unstable the cliff edge at the bottom of the garden was.

Only a few days after exchanging contracts at the auction, the cliff edge decided to relocate itself under the living room with the result that half the house and nearly all the garden ended up on its way down to or actually onto the beach many hundreds of feet below.

They did put up an argument not to complete the purchase but ultimately, they were forced to do so because what occurred could actually have been reasonably predicted to happen at any point and thus the geological fragility of the immediate vicinity was an intrinsic feature of the property.

A massively expensive purchase which became literally worthless, a true property nightmare. Lesson to self – don't bid blind!

Getting Stuck into Auction Viewings

By Jo Lines

On one of my first auction viewings as the agent in 2002, I became the victim of one a cover up. A small, terraced house I visited at 5pm in the evening on a cold and wet night in late autumn. It was getting dark as I turned up to the house. I had a massive bunch of keys from which it took me ages to find the front door key. I had turned up early to have a look around as it was my first time there.

It was a bit eerie to say the least, as I pushed the light switch nothing happened. No electricity – great I thought in a sarcastic tone! I proceeded to carefully check out this dark, dingy property. There was no furniture and looked like it had been empty for a very long time. I walked up the stairs to check out the bedrooms on the first floor, as I took each step it felt a bit wobbly, but I thought no more of it, until literally the half landing beneath me collapsed and my feet went through the floorboards!

This was literally my worst nightmare, stuck, in pain, in the dark and in a smelly old house. Panic set in! As I tried to wriggle out, it just made it worse, like fighting to escape quicksand. My saving grace was the fact that I had people viewing the property shortly. I waited for what felt like an eternity, shouting out in the hope that someone would hear me (I wish we had had mobile phones like we do now!) It was a block viewing, five minutes later, three people showed up to the property and thankfully the front door was not locked. With the help of them all, I managed to get out of the floor. I am pleased to say the property did sell at auction and I did visit again 18 months later after a new staircase had been put in and a full refurbishment done. What a transformation!

Lessons learnt:

- Always take a torch (or now mobile phone) on all viewings.
- Don't arrange a viewing for after dark in dodgy looking properties.
- Always be careful on the stairs and shout when things go wrong – people will help you in your time of need if you ask.

The Drive of No Return

By Anonymous

A client refused our advice in terms of auction purchases, and always seemed to bring the reply "I know what I am doing". The client's excitement prevailed and was barely containable subsequent to them winning the bid on a £862,000 property at auction unbeknown to us as the broker tasked with finding finance. "Wonderful value" was our client's response. Unfortunately, the lack of Planning and Building Regs was apparent within a couple of minutes when looking at the spec.

The successful purchase entailed a house built randomly in what one can only assume was the vendor's garden. The property boasted a very large flat roof, little or no natural light from the lack of windows, property access served only through a man-made cave via the neighbouring property without proper access rights.

It gets worse; a narrow unofficial drive through which can only be accessed once your car wing mirrors have been folded back, no room to turn around - meaning all those who entered the grounds never actually returned.

The 'drive of no return' existed only due to the rubble remaining from digging the access cave. There was no discernible garden, and the property was situated less than three feet from the front door of a house whose garden the property randomly occupied.

"Can we not get retrospective planning and building regs?" was the client's question. You can make up your own responses.

What it all added up to was that the property had zero value other than that of the current owner's garden land value once the property was demolished.

The client therefore lost their £86,200 deposit. We can only assume that the property has since been rightfully demolished.

Lessons we learned along the way:

- Do your due diligence before putting your hand up at auction.
- Under certain conditions akin to the ones above, losing £86,200 can very much feel like a 'win', when the only other viable option is bankruptcy. However, with the right guidance and due diligence prior to auction this whole sorry affair could've been easily avoided.
- Talk to your professional advisers before visiting an auction.

Chapter 2

Legals and Finance

Property Transaction Issue

By Andy Price

Property transactions can be problematic at the best of times; what with tight deadlines, tricky legal issues within a property's title and working with funders and other lawyers who can sometimes be less than helpful. You may wonder if there's a way to make it more complicated, and arguably there is – auction purchases.

Don't let this scare you too much – many auction purchases fly through to completion without a hitch, within the timescales set by the auction conditions and much more streamlined than a usual transaction. Exchange technically happens at the point at which the deposit is paid at auction, yet that is often where the problems arise – you can commit yourself to purchasing a property before your funder is in place or before your lawyer has considered the title and highlighted potential issues. Ultimately that comprises much of our role as lawyers; find the problems but then find a way to solve them to achieve the goal of completion.

Auction purchases can be very profitable and a great addition to an existing or a new property portfolio. Many of our investor clients source good deals at auctions which often in turn make great financial sense. However, any property transaction can be risky, but auction purchases can see large deposits on the line when problems arise.

Many of our clients instruct us to review the auction pack for a property before they bid at auction and therefore before they bind themselves to purchase it. The vendor's solicitor is under no obligation to answer or respond to any enquiries raised, although a purchaser's solicitor may make such enquiries in the best interest of their client. If a vendor refuses to answer any pre-auction enquiries, a purchaser may question 'why not?' Sometimes a refusal to give further information speaks louder than a willingness to give it up. Once a purchaser is successful at auction and the auction purchase conditions come into play, the vendor is even less likely to assist with any enquiries, perhaps such as those raised by a funder. It is therefore crucial to have everything in order before the auction.

A client approached us as they intended to purchase some flats, but not the freehold building, at an upcoming auction. We talked the client through the different options available, including instructing us to review the auction packs for the flats or how our work may be limited to just taking the transaction through to completion after the client was successful at auction. The client was keen for us to review the auction packs and legal documentation, however, was very passionate about how much of a good deal they would be getting, as the flats were rather cheap. After further discussions with the potential client, it transpired that they had already bid and been successful at the auction, committing themselves to complete the purchase of the flats in 28 days.

We confirmed with the client that we would assist with progressing the transaction to completion, which prompted the next question – how were they funding the balance of the purchase price? They had already parted with upwards of £97,000 in cash for the deposit. This is when the next problem became clear – they intended to use bridging funding. With 20 days left remaining of the 28-day completion deadline, the client confirmed that they had only just started the process with their broker for the bridging application, which left us very tight for time. We quickly became aware that there would be a third-party solicitor acting for the funder, so we began reviewing the paperwork in anticipation for their enquiries.

New leases were being granted for the flats, with the vendor remaining as the landlord and our client being the tenant. On review of the leases, it immediately became clear that they would not be compliant for a lender – the vendor's solicitor had drafted extremely unfair and expensive provisions for the service charge, introduced an additional management charge and the lease was silent on important provisions as to insurance and responsibility for the roof and structure. When raising this with the solicitor acting for the vendor, in the nicest way possible, we were hit by a complete brick wall. Technically speaking they had absolutely no obligation to help or assist by amending the leases, however you couldn't help but wonder whether they were being deliberately extra obstructive.

With a cash deposit of more than £97,000 on the line and a bridging lender to satisfy with non-compliant leases, at that point, the lightbulb moment happened – perhaps that is why the flats were so cheap and seemed like such a good deal. Hindsight is a wonderful thing; however, it was more important to find a way to resolve the situation for our client.

It was clear that we could not proceed with the leases as they were drafted. It would not be in the best interests of our client and it would never satisfy the funder or their solicitor. Funders can be very strict with their conditions for leasehold properties and are unlikely to compromise on the terms of the lease. It may have been possible to indemnify against the risk posed by the lease provisions, however in this case the leases had been newly drafted and were to be granted and then registered.

We had to reach a compromise with the vendor's solicitor, however it became clear that this was ultimately going to be at the cost of our client. We redrafted the leases to make them compliant and posed the underlying point to the vendor's solicitor – our client wanted to buy and their client wanted to sell, so we needed to find a way to meet this common goal. If the vendor's solicitor did not agree, our client would not be able to proceed to completion which would put them in breach of the auction conditions and they would forfeit their deposit. Our client decided that the cost of the extra work involved outweighed the risk of losing the deposit, and also the figures still stacked up when considering the future profit they could make. After much negotiation with the vendor's solicitor, an agreement for our client to pay an additional premium and an extension agreed to the auction conditions deadline, we were almost there. We had technically overcome the legal issue of the leases being non-compliant by redrafting them to the satisfaction of the funder, albeit at a cost to our client.

When considering auction purchases, given the risks and complexities of the potential legal issues involved, it is important to have your 'ducks in a row' and be as prepared as possible. As a purchaser, you will be in a much stronger position if the legal issues are identified prior to the auction, and always remember to question why the property is being sold at auction in the first place. If it was an easy and uncomplicated sale, it may have made more sense for it to have sold on the open market. That is not to say you can't get a fantastic deal at auction that progresses and completes smoothly, just ensure you have done your research first.

A Day in the Life of a Conveyancer

By Tishka Chapman

I became a Licensed Conveyancer because I wanted to specialise in this particular area of law which I find both challenging and motivating. In practical terms it is my role to ensure that all the documentation, contracts and financial arrangements associated with, for example, buying, selling, or re-mortgaging a residential property or piece of land are in order. However, the truth of the matter is that my role is not limited to legal practicalities of a property transaction, my job also includes acting as counsellor, therapist, arbitrator, peacemaker, and many other aspects of a job of a social worker!

Buyers and sellers travel through a roller coaster journey of mixed emotions during the course of the conveyancing transaction – I travel through this journey with each of my clients and I am there to share their excitement and anticipation and support them through their anxieties, worries and angst whether they are becoming a homeowner for the first time or selling a home for the last time to move into residential care.

Each conveyancing transaction is a unique experience for a conveyancer and each transaction is a story with its own tale of happiness, sadness, frustration and elation and everything in between!

I am always intrigued to receive the Memorandum of Sale and Sales Particulars from the Estate Agent at the beginning of a transaction. Even if the brief description of the property, (which includes every word available in the thesaurus to encourage and entice further reading) is sometimes a little too generous, i.e. the "original features" can include everything from the brass door knocker on the rotting front door that is desperately in need of replacement, to the cast iron bath with taps that you need a wrench to turn on and off! And a reference to "far-reaching views" is applicable if you stand on a chair in the attic room and peer through the skylight window! But what intrigues me the most is the photographs within the sales brochure.

Whilst I go to great lengths to report to my clients on the covenants and restrictions affecting the property, and ensure they are absolutely certain as to their responsibilities for maintaining the boundaries, and explain the expenditures they will be obliged to meet to maintain the shared or common areas defined by the lease or transfer, it never ceases to amaze me how insignificant these matters are, when clients contact me to ask to me questions such as:

- "Can the seller hear their neighbours?"
- "Are there any funny smells?"
- "Is the property haunted?"
- "Does the seller employ a gardener or cleaner and, if so, how much do they pay them?"

Yes, there are times when it is necessary to gently remind clients that I am instructed to deal with the legal work, but if the question is important to the client, then it has to be raised with the seller's solicitors – even if the response from the seller's solicitors is simply that they are not obliged to deal with enquiries that do not concern the legal title to the property!

I once had a client who moved twice in the same road; they loved the location but in the first property the neighbour smoked outside and the smoke came into their property through their window and they could not bear it! The second property was "better", but the neighbours were a bit on the "noisy side". Thankfully, my client stuck it out though!

I have been involved in lots of complex cases during my time in conveyancing and one case, in particular, involved clients who had inherited an unregistered property that had been in their family for generations.

The estate agent believed there was a potential issue with the title, as it appeared that part of the land which should have been included in the title, appeared to have been incorporated and registered as part of the neighbouring land.

As a conveyancer, I am not, of course, a surveyor, but having undertaken a site visit, it was apparent from the layout of the property on the physical ground that this was indeed the case. I made an application to the Land Registry to rectify this issue which involved the Land Registry's surveyor attending the property themselves to draw up an accurate plan. The process took a period of 4-5 months to finally resolve to enable the property to be marketed for sale. As the issue was resolved in advance of the property being marketed for sale, my client was able to proceed with the sale in the full knowledge that the transaction would proceed without delay.

This is a good example of the benefit to a seller of instructing a conveyancer as soon as they make the decision to sell their property as opposed to waiting for an offer to be made before appointing a conveyancer – the conveyancer can check the title to the property in advance and highlight and address any issues without the parties to the transaction becoming frustrated by delays.

Another matter involved an elderly owner who had moved into a care home. Their family was acting as seller in their capacity as attorneys for the elderly owner. The property was unregistered, and the deeds were nowhere to be found! After enquiries were made to other local firms and the banks failing to identify the location of the deeds, the only option I had was to reconstruct the title to the property by collating evidence including historical correspondence, photographs and Statutory Declarations from neighbours and the elderly owner. This process took several months to conclude, but luckily the Land Registry were happy with the evidence provided and granted a Qualified Title – we also provided indemnity insurance to the buyer to support this.

There have been many occasions when buyers and sellers come to arrangements and agreements between themselves directly and have failed to advise me. They clearly do not appreciate the impact of these discussions and the potential for these matters to lead to a dispute between them, until they begin to fall out with their buyer/ seller and the transaction becomes contentious and the clients become fraught. Clients appear to rely on their conveyancer to resolve these disputes as part of the conveyancing transaction!

In summary, a career as a lawyer specialising in conveyancing is very challenging and diverse but, most of all, it is very rewarding, requiring compassion and understanding. I could not necessarily describe a "typical" day at work because the simple fact is that no two days, no two transactions and no two clients are ever the same!

Super Rapid Completion

By Dave Ottley

Scenario A

I would ask you to picture the scene as follows:

- We had just moved our businesses onto new offices in 2019.
- Our business levels were busy, and we were awash with sorting IT issues and other related moving challenges.
- We received a call from a customer who had previously used our services.
- They had agreed to purchase a light refurbishment project and had paid a deposit, having been assured that the funding would not be an issue.
- Three days before exchange the funder declined to proceed as the valuation report had raised concerns about the comparison re-sale values once completed.
- Effectively they were now unable to complete the purchase and faced losing their deposit.

We quickly moved into action and requested all relevant documentation for the case including the valuation. Working late into the evening to prepare a new funding pack to go to relevant members of our funding panel for their consideration, we made a large number of phone calls to ensure the case was looked at immediately rather than after the weekend, as time was of the essence to stop the deal collapsing.

By utilising our knowledge of the local area and our funders we were able to obtain a funding offer the same day and arranged the on-site valuation on the Monday morning.

Fortunately, the case was well prepared and with a collaborative effort from all parties saw the deal complete by the following Friday.

Happily, the project was completed within five months and the re-sale valuation was achieved due to the high quality of the light refurbishment. This saw the lender repaid in full, the client extremely happy and moving onto their next project.

Points for consideration:

- An Agreement in Principle is not a confirmed offer of funding.
- Always make sure that your lender is fully committed to a deal, prior to instructing legal processes.
- Make sure you and/or your broker stays in daily contact with the lender to ensure issues can be highlighted and reviewed/ resolved without delays.
- Remember the phrase "Facta Non Verba" on every deal – "Deeds not words".

Zero Valuation

By Dave Ottley

Scenario B

- We were approached for a business loan by a client, who wished to secure it against a holiday let property that was unencumbered.
- The property was of non-standard construction and whilst it was in a beauty spot, it had been allocated a value of nil for mortgage purposes by the funder they had approached.
- This left the client in the unenviable situation of being unable to raise the funds that they desperately needed to support their separate trading business.
- The property was being marketed for sale and this was the loan repayment source.

Our clients were extremely worried and concerned that their trading business could fail, and we faced a tough task with the NIL mortgage value, however we contacted two local funders and discussed the case in some detail with them.

One of these funders visited our offices the next day to review all the information and went to visit the property to carry out their own valuation.

They were able to view the application favourably and issued a formal offer letter within 24 hours to enable the loan to proceed.

The legal process proved complicated with the non-standard security and many questions were raised of a complicated nature, however working closely with the funder and solicitors on both sides, the case was completed within four weeks.

Points for consideration:

- When dealing in properties with non-standard construction or have certain restrictions e.g. Holiday restrictions, Grade II listed building etc, it is vital to prepare a full pack of information for funders at the outset, so that any potential issues are identified at an early stage.
- This is especially important to ensure that valuers have relevant information, prior to paying their fees to avoid duplicate costs and late notification of issues.
- In this case the first lender instructed was via an online search and the key consideration for the client initially was to go for the cheapest rates and fees package.
- This highlights the saying the "the bitterness of poor service lasts long after the sweetness of cheap pricing has passed".

Bridging Loan Nightmare

By Roy Inman

It was November 2011 and if you had been in County Court you would have seen me sat with a commercial litigation solicitor and barrister both working for me at a combined hourly rate of over £600 and we'd been there for over two hours waiting already. Those two hours just sitting waiting had just cost me over £1,200 and I had no idea how much more it was going to cost me or if I could potentially end up losing my whole property portfolio worth over £3.5 Million that had taken me nearly nine years to build. I was very scared; we were taking on one of the largest legal services businesses in the world.

Just over two years earlier, just before the recession, I was investing heavily in property and had purchased four investment properties at the same time with a small bridging company that I had a great relationship and loan terms with. Although the rate was quite high at 1.5% pcm they would lend me 100% of the purchase price with the loan being no more than 80% of the survey valuation.

For example, if the surveyor valued the property at £100,000, they would lend me £80,000, and if I was paying £80,000 for the property, they would lend me the full purchase price. Now, this was all great, it allowed me to purchase property on short term funding and then if any work needed doing, I would complete the refurbishment and then refinance onto much more favourable, cheaper long term mortgage finance.

However, just before the recession fully kicked in, I'd purchased four properties using this bridging finance structure and when it came time to re-mortgage them, one got stuck on the bridging finance. When I say, 'got stuck' what I really mean is that this was the first time in nine years of investing that I'd seen or experienced the 'Big Surveyor Down Value'. Surveyors may not value the property at what you would like all the time and may come in a little under what you hoped for, but this was huge on a property that was easily worth

£60,000 and I'd had valued at £65,000 3-4 months earlier (before refurbishment) when I purchased it and paid £44,000, he valued it at £40,000 which didn't even meet the lenders minimum valuation of £50,000.

Now this was a pain as I only needed the value to come in at £50,000 the re-mortgage would have gone through and everything would be fine. Luckily, I had a great relationship with this small bridging company. They knew I had about 40 properties with a great combined cashflow and covering the difference between the rent, which was £400 a month and the bridging finance costs at £660 month, wouldn't be a problem and allowed me to roll the bridging on until such times as I could refinance.

The lending I had on this property was only £44,000, It wasn't a huge amount of money, but I didn't want to be paying it off and owning the property outright and tying all the money up if I could help it. All lending kind of dried up, surveyors were down valuing everything and there was just a real problem in the market obtaining finance, so I decided to leave it and it ticked over nicely.

It was now August 2011, I received a letter from a law firm informing me that the bridging company had gone into administration (yes the property had been on bridging for over two years, I had it down valued three times by different surveyors in this time) and that according to the very limited records they had received from the bridging company they believed that I had not made a payment for over two years and that after adding the non-payment default interest to the original £44,000 borrowed I now owed £105,820. If this wasn't cleared, they would apply to the courts for a receiver to be appointed. I knew I had never missed a payment and if you're like me, you would have thought this was just a misunderstanding that could easily be sorted, how wrong was I!

After some digging, I discovered that the bridging company had been sold (something I had no idea of) to another business owner who had their fingers in far too many pies. They were not managing the bridging company at all and although I had made the payments fully up to date, the other bridging loans however were much larger than mine at £250,000 or more and they were not making their payment, this had sent the company into administration.

As I mentioned, I'd never missed a payment and saw this as a misunderstanding that could easily be resolved, and once resolved, I would look to clear the £44,000 loan. However, after having an initial conversation with them, providing all the information they requested, things went quiet and as far as I was concerned, I was waiting for them to confirm that the outstanding loan balance was the original £44,000 I had borrowed and then I could make the payment to close the account, job done. What I didn't want to do was make the £44,000 payment and for them to say that there is still an outstanding balance of £61,820, plus any costs they wanted to add on top.

Then around two months later, I received a letter from them with a court date that was just over two weeks away applying to the court to take the property into receivership. All along they just ignored everything I had said to them and had fully intended to apply for receivership, probably because they would make considerably more money this way. My biggest worry now was that they would take control of the property, badly manage it and add ridiculous levels of charges and costs on top of the £105,820 that they believed that I owed. They would then sell the property for way below market value and then look to come after me for the remaining balance, which at that point would have been way over £100,000 even after selling the property. Once they found out that I had a large property portfolio, God knows how much damage they could have done until they recovered the money and this really scared me. After all the hard work I had put in to get to this point all I could think was that I could lose everything.

As you can imagine, getting this letter was very stressful and caused many sleepless nights. After a few days of severe worry I had to make a decision. My back was against the wall and I could stay there and let them take the property and anything else they wanted or I could come out fighting and protect everything I had built and fighting is what I chose to do!

I tried to speak to everyone I knew about the best way forward but nobody could help. I researched online and finally came to the conclusion that I needed to speak to a Commercial Litigation Solicitor, so I spoke to any solicitors I knew to see if they could recommend anyone but that was a dead end.

I called up a couple of Commercial Litigation Solicitors, had an initial conversation with them and decided to instruct Agamemnon. After a lengthy conversation going through all the events leading up to this point Agamemnon came to the conclusion that I'd basically been grouped into the rest of the cases and caught up and treated the same as the bad bunch and that the administrators had not looked at it properly. He requested that I send across a detailed statement right from initial purchase through to current day along with any documents that would act as evidence. Two days later, a 16-page personal statement and all the evidence I could find I sent it across for him to review.

Time was getting tight now and we had less than a week until the court date where all the cases under the bridging company would be heard, not just mine. It wasn't as if we could even get it moved, changed, or postponed.

Agamemnon also had a conversation with a barrister he knew who specialised in this area and felt could really help. This meant I was now footing the cost of both a commercial litigation solicitor and a barrister. After reviewing the case the barrister had found a few holes in the way they had gone about applying for receivership, effectively they'd cut a lot of corners thinking no one would be standing up and defending their case, but boy were they wrong.

We pulled everything together and submitted the case, and there we sat in the court waiting to be called in. We had a couple of angles, one being all the evidence and the second being the incorrect application process the administrators had taken.

The time had come and we were called in, I was told to sit at the back and effectively keep my mouth shut and let my barrister handle it and for once I did exactly as I was told. My barrister went in with all guns blazing on all the areas that the administrators had done wrong in the application and this worked very well, too well in fact, the judge began to consider throwing the whole application out which was not what we wanted and certainly wasn't what the administrators wanted. Most of the other defendants hadn't even turned up and any that had actually made any sort of defence had only sent their solicitor acting on their behalf and were probably all guilty of pulling me into this mess in the first place. My barrister requested for our case to be looked at separately in isolation and not to apply it to the whole application due to the circumstances and the mountain of evidence we had submitted for our case.

After a little back and forth with my barrister presenting the case and evidence and the administrators conceding that they had not gone through all the 57 pages of evidence, the administrators agreed to adjourn for three months to give them time to go through all the evidence and potentially come to an agreement out of court. We had won the battle, but we hadn't yet won the war.

It was leading up to Christmas now and after a lot of correspondence we still didn't know what was going to happen, we were still waiting to get a final redemption figure after the administrators had reviewed through all the evidence. This is the last thing you want to be dealing with at any time in your life, but certainly not over Christmas. There had already been a lot of sleepless nights over the last 2-3 months and I didn't want it ruining Christmas as well.

Finally just before Christmas they came back with a redemption figure agreeing to accept the original £44,000 that I owed on the condition it was repaid before 18th January.

I can't describe the relief I had at that moment of receiving this news, I could relax and more important I could enjoy Christmas with my wife and two daughters Grace and Layla. My total legal bill came to over £10,000 and a lot of people ask me if I got that back from the other side. If I'm honest, at the time, it was the last thing I was thinking about and my solicitor never mentioned it. I was just glad to have my life back, that it was all done and over with. I was able to focus my time, effort, and energy on positive things to grow my business and to be properly present with my family again.

Although this was something that I'd been pulled into unintentionally and the chances of it happening to you are slim, my advice would be to make sure that you've got a really strong and tight exit strategy and potentially have a plan A, plan B and even a plan C if you're going to be using any short-term funding, whether it's JV funding, lending from friends, family, investors or bridging finance.

The Sex Dungeon and the Church

By Angelos Sanders

It is not every day that the church decide to get involved with a property purchase, but that is what happened with this particular purchase.

The scenario was that I was buying a property from a difficult seller and did not really need any further complications, but that is exactly what happened.

Among the myriad of difficulties the seller kept throwing my way, it was revealed that there was something interesting in the basement and that I should keep an open mind.

I arranged a viewing and went down with the estate agent (to the basement). We entered into this unknown part of the building which had such intrigue attached. I walked through the rotten wooden door and was hit by a terrible smell of something rotten and bad damp; you could literally taste it. Initially, there was just a to room in the basement with old tools scattered here, there, and everywhere. Nothing too shocking to see yet.

The room ahead had black painted walls and you needed to turn left to enter the other room. Onward I walked armed with my phone torch with a deep sense of curiosity. I turned the corner and there was no natural light as all the windows had been covered up, but I could see a dodgy old light switch. I flicked the switch and about two or three flickering candle lights illuminated the room slightly with their dull glow.

The walls were covered in a faded maroon coloured paint. My attention was drawn to the red leather chair with sharp metal decorated spikes at the top. I looked to the left-hand side of the room and there was a metal cage with bars so its occupants could not escape. Various other paraphernalia was scattered around the room, including a device that looked like an old radio with two dials. Upon closer inspection the dials showed electrical power output with connectors onto various parts of the body. There was also a long cylindrical black rubber object there, God knows what that was, perhaps a pointing device?

I took a few photos for the obligatory before and after portfolio document I produce at the end of every refurb I do and departed for daylight and fresh air again; fortunately my phone does not have a UV light – can you imagine the horrors!

Late into the conveyancing process, a church contacted the estate agent and asked what my intentions were with the building, specifically the basement. My initial reaction was, what in Heaven's name does this building have to do with the church, let alone what business is it of theirs what my intentions are? Good Lord, what I did with my property refurbs was my business only! Sweet Jesus, imagine if they were going to redecorate the inside of a church and I stuck my nose in and asked them what their intentions were with the redecoration?

They eventually dropped the inquisition and I was "permitted" to continue the purchase, not that there was any real danger of them slowing things down.

One wonders what their curiosity was with this particular property. Was it because the property had a bit of a reputation and they wanted to know if the upcoming refurb involved dismantling the interesting basement or was there another reason? Who knows? Either way, the dungeon has been decommissioned and the now sanitised basement is a storage area with its dungeon days long gone.

Underwriting Frustrations

By Anonymous

Many of our frustrations come from financing multi tenanted and HMO properties as they are complex.

A lender declined a case because on the product we had applied for it stated that only four bedrooms could be let, and four bedrooms were only currently being let. However the lender surmised that this property had the potential to be let as a 5-bedroom HMO. Upon further investigation the potential additional 'bedroom' in question actually transpired to be a utility room in between the kitchen and the backdoor which had a small table and single chair in it.

When challenged, the lender they stated that although this room couldn't be used as a bedroom, as it had a table and chair in it, they were classing it as a second communal room meaning the other communal room (the one where more than one person could be at a time) could be used as a 5th bedroom pushing it outside of their criteria.

Despite the room at the back of the house being under the legal-size limit, and the property already being licensed for a maximum of four occupants, the lender stood by their decision to decline and we had to find a new home for the case.

Another application was declined by a lender with similar 4-bedroom maximum criteria, because it had the potential for a loft conversion, which could make it a 5 bed HMO which would need a licence. The client had owned the house for 20+ years and never looked to convert the loft in that time and prior bank statements indicated the four-tenant history of the property.

Banks Do and Say the Funniest things

By Anonymous

- One lender confirmed that upon reviewing the customer's rental bank statements, that since they received the rental income via a letting agent rather than direct from the tenant - they would insist upon a gift letter being signed by their letting agent! We pointed out that it wasn't usual for a letting agents trying to turn a profit to gift monies to a landlord when it was rightfully theirs in the first place!
- Packager - "We have the client's (British) passport copy here; can you confirm that they have permanent rights to reside?"
- Lender - "We cannot lend anything on this residential case, because once the clients dividends are taken, there is no profit left to support the loan." Of course we all know that dividends are taken after profit is declared, i.e. *dividends do not diminish profit, they are paid from profit.*
- We called a lender to check on the progress of a product transfer (a switch to a new deal with the very same lender), the reply came "Does the client already have lending with us?"
- New lender on launching into the Ltd company SPV lending market. "We do not accept Directors Loans for deposit funds, the client must sign a gift letter indicating that they are gifting their deposit funds to the Ltd Company" Therefore requiring tax to be paid on the drawings of the loan! That stance has since changed.

And the best one in my opinion.

We applied for a standard single let BTL mortgage on a standard single let property. The application was accepted and valued as being in order by the RICS qualified surveyor. The underwriter doing their final pre-underwriting checks, went onto RightMove to view the property and declined the property declaring that it was an HMO, which they wouldn't allow. The lender was concerned that since there were 'locks on internal doors' the property bore all the hallmarks of an HMO which their criteria forbids. Viewing the offending photos ourselves, the lock was, in fact, on an ensuite bathroom.

After a week of challenging the lender, the response came; "It does look like a bathroom door bearing in mind the tiles." It was eventually overturned by the bank's chief surveyor.

The Hidden (Forgotten) Costs of Property Buying

By Peter Hill

As a Chartered Accountant with almost 40 years' experience, I have worked with clients on hundreds of purchases or sales of property. Some of these have been for tens of millions and some for as little as £50k. These are capable business owners advised by good lawyers and funded by reputable banks. There have been a number of situations where a last-minute surprise almost scuppered the deal.

Over the years, the transaction tax known as stamp duty has been a bit of a political football, with various governments seeing it as a soft target for revenue raising or as a lever for social engineering by punishing those owning multiple properties to give first time owner occupiers an advantage.

Regardless of your political opinions, stamp duty can add a big number to any transaction.

You would think that it would be an issue raised early in the negotiations and funding discussions so that the calculation of the full charge and the timing of payment would be known well before exchange occurs.

However, I think it is reasonable to suggest that maybe 5% of those transactions got to within a few days of exchange when a major issue was uncovered. The lawyers started asking for details of where all the funds were coming from for the purchase and sent a draft completion statement which showed all the transaction costs as well as the purchase price, and of course the stamp duty.

This has then prompted the buyer to panic as they had failed to consider this cost and did not have the funds to pay it.

In a few of these situations the funders have been able to lend a bit more because the loan to value (LTV) was OK, but on others the funding was maxed out. On at least two occasions, the vendor has had to agree to a partial payment of the proceeds with a bit more to follow, so that the buyer could pay the stamp duty. Some deals have simply failed because already stretched buyers had no way to finance the stamp duty charge, and the vendor wouldn't budge.

The rules are clear, the calculations quite simple, but this is still forgotten about until really close to exchange, in a number of cases.

There is a similar issue with VAT. Some properties may be subject to the additional 20% VAT charge if they have been 'opted to tax'. This is, of course, a much bigger number than stamp duty rates, so more than a few deals have hit a serious problem when the VAT charge was discovered late in the transaction. Often this can be fixed with a temporary loan, repayable once the next VAT return is filed and the VAT refunded, but even this may change the plans for the transaction if the buyer is not VAT registered (Financial advisors for example).

The largest case I have seen was a care home conversion on a property for about £2M. The buyer, used to buying property without VAT, was buying from a local authority that simply didn't understand VAT. A week before completion the issue was raised, effectively just adding 20% to the cost of the building as the buyer was an exempt business for VAT purposes and would not be able to recover it.

In this case the £400k of VAT was a potential deal breaker for both sides.

The conclusion was that any buyer of the property was likely to encounter the same problem (it was a care home likely to be sold for that purpose), so that no one would pay £2m + VAT, and the vendor therefore conceded that the £2m would need to be inclusive of VAT. A big drop in proceeds for the vendor.

On both these issues, the transaction structure and costs should have been identified much earlier in the deal, to avoid progressing with a deal that will not work, or last-minute panics with the associated delays and costs that these bring.

Frustrating Finance

By Jackie Tomes

We all know that banks can be a nightmare, particularly when it comes to ironing out the small details and making sure you've ticked all their boxes. But from my experience the bankers aren't the worst part of the finance process; it's the bank's solicitors!

The problem I've found is that often banks can be reasoned with and they understand how to take a view on more unusual situations. Unfortunately, they also need to have the thumbs up from their own legal representation, because without it they are at risk of potentially invalidating their insurances or violating their own borrowing conditions. This leaves you at the mercy of whichever law firm the bank has chosen to represent them. I've found that the worst lawyers are those who only see in black and white and can't comprehend that they might not know everything, even within areas that are nothing to do with law!

My finance nightmare occurred at the end of a project that had required several planning permissions. I was refinancing from a bridge onto a long-term product, but both products were with the same bank, so I didn't anticipate there being any problems as they had already vetted everything when agreeing the bridge. The problems began when the bank's solicitors started asking questions about the new internal layouts.

They were asking why the internal layouts that were agreed in our planning permission were different to the actual internal layouts we had ended up with, and more specifically why there was a whole extra flat that had not been drawn in the submitted plans. Now I wouldn't begrudge you from thinking to yourself that this was in fact a very valid question, and potentially a clear indication that we were in breach of our planning permission. However, that's because you aren't yet in possession of all the facts, which is more than can be said for the bank's solicitor, who most certainly had every fact they needed to be able to solve this riddle themselves.

You see, I had three different planning permissions for this project. Two of these were under permitted development rights and these specifically related to the internal layouts. The last one was under full planning and only related to the external changes being made to the building. The issue was that I had originally submitted for planning under permitted development to turn the building into three flats, and at the same time I submitted the full planning application for the external changes we needed to make. Six months later I realised we could fit another flat in the building and so applied again under permitted development rights to add a fourth flat. This was why there were three different planning permissions.

Unfortunately due to the change of plan halfway through, no single one of our applications had the final correct layout on it, meaning you needed to understand the detail of what each application was for, as well as the chronology of when applications had been submitted, in order to see the full picture of exactly what had been granted. Clearly not simple, but most certainly something that you'd expect an experienced property lawyer who primarily works on commercial property cases, has years of experience dealing with complex planning permissions and has on hand the full experience of a commercial bank who also deal with this type of thing on a daily basis, to be able to work out.

Well, for some reason this lawyer ignored the bigger picture of the multiple planning permissions and decided that in his opinion the only floorplans that officially applied were in fact the only ones that weren't even relevant. He only cared about the ones included in the application for external changes to the building and ignored all the others. The most stupid thing is that these floorplans weren't even the ones that I had ever considered using, as they were just the very first ideas that had been drawn up by our draftsman, and as the internal layouts weren't officially part of the application itself, these floorplans shouldn't have even been included in the application.

After 2-3 weeks of argument with this computer-says-no lawyer, and several very convincing emails sent over to him from our planning consultant, he refused to relent on his position and stubbornly insisted that the only solution he would consider was for me to make another application to amend that one planning permission so that it included the correct floorplans; another 8–10-week application process!

In the end I was stuck on that bridge for 10 weeks longer than I should have been all because of one obtuse lawyer, costing me an unnecessary extra £6,000 in interest payments.

The Importance of Getting a Report on Title

By Verona Cocks

This story demonstrates the importance of getting a report on title even when you consider you are very familiar with the property.

Sometime ago, I acted for a corporate client who was the owner of the freehold of a number of flats and whose director had been a leaseholder for a number of years. Unfortunately, there was no express clause in the lease and no other provisions in the management company's articles or other agreement requiring the management company to seek consent from the landlord before carrying out works to the freehold. The landlord's director whilst a leaseholder, was not a member of the management company. The building itself was also a listed building to which works were required and for which an application for listed building consent was required to be made to the local authority.

The management company had made such an application without giving the requisite notice to the landlord under the listed buildings legislation and there was no other recourse under the lease. Whilst a complaint could be made to the local authority for them to take enforcement action, whether they did or not was within their discretion and this brought other issues with it. The landlord remained ultimately responsible for those works and basically did not have any control over them.

As it was, the landlord sold the freehold which resolved the position, but the other solution would be to make an application to the First-tier Tribunal for variation of the terms of the leases under the provisions of the Landlord and Tenant Act 1987 on the grounds that the lease fails to make satisfactory provision for the repair or maintenance of the flats, the building containing the flats. A report on title on the purchase of the freehold ought to have revealed this issue and then any such rectification could have been factored into the purchase price.

Contract Law Issue

By Andy Price

When Contract Law is mentioned, your first thought might be that of a snail in a bottle of ginger beer. A close second may be that when you consider property sales and purchases, the contract is at the heart of the transaction. It reflects the terms of the transaction as agreed between the parties, dictates their obligations, and provides a remedy in circumstances when things don't go as planned. Whether it be an entirely bespoke contract or a precedent incorporating the Standard Conditions of Sale as implemented by The Law Society, provided it is drafted correctly the contract can be the key to protecting your position if matters take a turn for the worse.

Contracts which may be considered more straightforward, perhaps such as those for simple residential sales and purchases, are vital when dealing with, what is perhaps, one of the stressful events in life for many people – moving house.

What happens if one of the parties cannot complete after exchange? What if the balance of the purchase price will not be received in time for the agreed completion date? What happens if the property is struck by lightning between exchange and completion? These questions can be answered by referring to the conditions within the contract. Equally, complex contracts which may contain option agreements, condition precedents and provisions for retentions require accurate drafting to ensure that the contract is as balanced as possible between the vendor and the purchaser.

A client was proposing to enter into a conditional contract to purchase a parcel of land that formed part of a field in an area prime for investment. The client was experienced in development and had an existing professional relationship with many of the neighbouring landowners, but not the particular vendor in this case. However, our client was in discussion with the vendor to purchase this parcel of land as part of a wider context; there were a number of different transactions taking place all on different terms between the same parties.

The land was being sold with detailed planning permission that had already been obtained by the vendor to build seventeen detached dwellings and an office block. This was part of the attraction for our client, being a self-build developer and both the cost and the benefit of the planning permission were factored into the purchase price. The vendor was also very familiar with this type of development, and in fact spent considerable time discussing the planning permission with our client, including how the final permission came to be granted by the local Council and on what basis they had applied for that specific type of dwelling. The contract was agreed and then exchanged with completion being conditional on a number of factors, including our client obtaining satisfactory soil reports, the utility connections being provided and the other transactions between the parties hitting specific milestones.

Between exchange and completion our client began preparing for development, so work could begin as soon as possible after completion. Our client instructed their surveyor, and in accordance with the provisions of the contract and the planning permission, began initial work such as soil tests and topographical reports. Unfortunately, at this point things began to unravel. Our client's surveyor became aware that the planning permission that had been obtained was in fact completely inappropriate for the land, and to be blunt, completely useless. The boundaries of the planning permission plans did not match those on the ground, there were inconsistencies with the shape of the parcel of land being conveyed and it was clear that the seventeen dwellings and office block detailed in the planning permission would not actually fit on the land itself. Clearly this was an issue – one of the main things, if not *the* main thing, that attracted our client to the deal was that it was being sold with the planning permission having already been obtained. It was now apparent that it was not physically possible to implement that planning permission, completely changing the value of the land to our client.

You may wonder why our client had not instructed their surveyor to carry out such investigations and that is perhaps a fair question, given the well-established concept in property transactions of 'caveat emptor' – 'buyer beware.' This was reinforced to our client as part of our due diligence report prior to exchange. However, applying that principle on such a broad basis may be flawed in these circumstances, when considering the relationship between our client and the vendor. The issue being that our client and the vendor had spent considerable time prior to exchange discussing the various transactions between them, the development of the land and in particular the planning permission. Our client had relied on what the vendor had told them about the planning permission and their assertions about their expertise in this area, but unfortunately, it then became difficult for the vendor to provide our client with answers to the questions that had now arisen.

On that basis, it was then considered that these circumstances were entering into the realm of Misrepresentation – a specialist area of Contract Law. Had a false representation been made by the vendor regarding the planning permission which induced our client to enter into the contract? There were many technical points to consider, including how, when, why and with what knowledge the vendor had provided the information to our client. Our client had relied on these representations, but this was clearly bridging the gap between conveyancing and litigation and would be considered out of the scope of a standard property transaction.

An important point to remember – although a contract can provide an appropriate remedy, very often the aggrieved party will need to take litigious action and sue the defaulting party based on the terms of the contract, rather than simply relying on the terms themselves. This can be costly (although costs are very often also dealt with within the contract) but a war of words can quickly ensue, whereas the intention of the parties in this case remained to get the deal over the line. However it was clear the contract would need to be renegotiated. Thankfully in this situation, the parties were keen to resolve the situation.

Completion had not yet taken place, and none of the condition precedents had yet been triggered which would have left our client with no choice but to either be in default or complete. Our client could have relied on the termination provisions within the contract and no longer be bound by its terms. However, this was arguably not appropriate in this case, given that this transaction formed part of a number of other agreements between the parties. Our client agreed that perhaps the best course of action was to enter into a variation to the contract, which introduced a further condition precedent regarding receipt of amended planning permission from the local council and dealt with amending the financial aspects of the transaction.

It was fortunate that in this instance that a resolution could be met between the parties without dissecting the contract in court. The contract was crucial both before and after the issues with the planning permission became apparent, and the parties had to be flexible to ensure that the contract ultimately reflected a viable transaction. The original contract allowed for subsequent variations, which ensured that the appropriate amendments could be made to reflect the changed terms, and the parties did not get embroiled in a technical contractual dispute.

Sometimes the contract can get a little forgotten, particularly when the focus for many of our investor clients is often profitability and securing the best deal for their portfolio. However it is undoubtedly crucial to remember the importance of the contract and how it fits in the bigger picture of what you are trying to achieve. Rather than worrying about things going wrong, think of how they could be resolved using the terms of the contract in the event that they do go wrong. Or failing that, just think of that snail in the ginger beer bottle.

Trying to Break a Contract and the Consequences

By Darren Clegg

At the time of the 2008 UK recession, I was acting for a developer specialising in new-build city centre apartments. The market had previously been extremely buoyant and there were around 200+ flats under construction where contracts for sale had been exchanged 'off-plan' in readiness for completion later. Some flats had been sold to owner-occupiers, but most had been reserved by wealthy buy to let owners with large portfolios. Due to the sudden decline in property values, with city centre flats hit hardest, most of the purchasers refused to complete because the flats were now worth around 30% less than the contract price.

My clients sought my advice. I told them to issue Court proceedings against each purchaser who was refusing to complete, seeking specific performance of the sale contract with damages in the alternative. We issued approximately 69 claims over a period of three months. The purchasers initially banded together to fight the claims alleging misrepresentation and other failures by the developer, but over time their interests diverged and slowly but surely each purchaser approached my developer clients wishing to settle before the claims went to trial.

Sometimes my clients would agree to sweeten the deal by including a furniture package if the purchaser agreed to complete quickly, but with the threat of the Court action continuing if the purchaser refused. This combination of carrot and stick produced results and in the end only a very small number of purchasers did not complete at the original contract price in most instances because they were owner-occupiers unable to secure a mortgage. They were still required to pay Court costs and damages. The action we took kept my clients afloat during the worst of the recession and persuaded their bankers not to foreclose on their loans. Prospective purchasers of property need to appreciate that once contracts have been exchanged, the seller can go to Court to compel the purchaser to complete at the contract price and the Courts have supported such action, irrespective of whether the value of the property has increased or decreased during the period of construction.

Chapter 3

Purchase Surveys

The House that Frightened the Purchasers and Surveyors

By Stuart Hallworth

This story occurred during an inspection for a mortgage valuation, which can be very quick, lasting as little as 20 minutes, depending on the size of the property. Their purpose is to advise the lender on things that could affect their security and provide an opinion of Market Value. They do not amount to a survey of the property, yet the majority of people who buy with a mortgage rely on the Mortgage Valuation Report in the belief that it is a survey. They have little idea of how brief the inspection is and that only issues that are important to the lender get reported.

These days, I prefer to work with clients who want a proper survey and need to know the surveyor is working with just their interests in mind. Around half of my clients are property investors and being a property investor myself, I am in a good position to advise them from an investor's point of view.

One investor client asked me to carry out the RICS HomeBuyer Report at a property which was now on the market at an attractive price, as two previous sales had fallen through due to structural movement. The Homebuyer involves a much more detailed inspection lasting 2 – 3 hours or more, depending on the size of the property.

This particular property was empty, old fashioned and due for complete refurbishment. Externally, I could not see any sign of structural movement that was of a serious or progressive nature. Nor was there any at ground floor level on the inside. There was some dampness, rot attack and other issues, but not structural movement. Next, I went upstairs. In the rear bedroom there were huge cracks crossing the chimney breast, extending into the walls either side. There was no obvious cause.

In a Mortgage Valuation inspection, upon seeing the cracks, the surveyor would have just referred the case to a structural engineer for further investigation. The mortgage lender would have been unwilling to proceed until an engineer had been appointed and a report issued, either confirming stability or recommending acceptable remedial works. This involves an additional expense, which many buyers would not have been willing to pay, especially if they were first time buyers and there were other similar properties available at the same time.

As the cracking was restricted to the top corner of the building, I knew that it was unlikely to be a symptom of subsidence and the source was probably going to be connected to the roof, so I needed to get into the roof space. The access hatch was in the top of an integral cupboard, which was obstructed by a shelf at high level, which meant that getting access was going to be difficult. Within the confines of a Mortgage Valuation, the surveyor wouldn't have taken the trouble to get past the obstruction and probably reported that the loft could not be accessed. However, in a HomeBuyer inspection, I needed to make more effort, especially as the roof space was holding the answer to the question of what caused the cracking. I leant the ladders against the shelf, climbed up, carefully manoeuvred myself over the shelf and lifted the loft access hatch.

The torchlight revealed modern underlay beneath the roof tiles, which would not have been there when the house was built. The roof must have received a comprehensive overhaul in the recent past. The rear chimney breast was water stained and there were huge damp stains over the main roof beams adjacent. This was evidence that a lot of water had been leaking in. There was no sign of a hole and logic determined that the roof overhaul must have been necessary to repair the leak. Back in the bedroom below, I tested the chimney breast and walls for damp with the moisture detector, but all surfaces were dry.

Fitting the evidence together, the conclusion was that the roof or chimney flashing had leaked in the past, allowing water to run down the face of the chimney breast. It must have continued for some time, leading to saturation of the chimney masonry, and extending into the adjoining walls. Then the leak was repaired, allowing the saturated masonry to dry out. As it did so, it shrank, causing the plaster to crack, giving the impression that the building had moved, when it hadn't. The damage was largely cosmetic and could be remedied by filling or replastering, prior to redecorating.

This story shows that if the previous purchasers had arranged a survey as opposed to relying on the mortgage valuation report, they would have had a chance of proceeding with the purchase and the vendor would have achieved a better sale price. However, in the end, it meant that my client was able to proceed instead, paying less for the property and probably getting a better return on their investment. It also illustrates that if you are an investor, looking for properties that have fallen through due to adverse mortgage valuation reports, this could enable you to buy more properties at more advantageous prices, but always do your due diligence before completing any purchase.

The Value of a Survey and Why it Pays to Keep Your Mouth Shut

By Peter Hill

The first property I bought was a first floor one bedroom flat, for the princely sum of £22,500.

The market was rising fast, as was my income, so I decided to move on within 18 months, selling it for £42,500. Pretty good return, but that was the mid 80's!

Before I marketed the flat, I decorated it with a lick of paint and some new carpets, and it was quickly snapped up by an elderly person who was downsizing having lost their partner. They visited with their daughter and loved it. I asked if they needed a survey for a mortgage, and they explained that they were a cash buyer so there was no need.

The deal proceeded quickly and easily, with completion in about a month.

Unfortunately, about four months later, I received a legal letter saying I was to be sued for misrepresentation, as the flat had a serious dry and wet rot problem that would require most of the floor (ground floor ceiling) to be replaced and some walls taken back to brick work.

The accusation was that I had persuaded the buyer not to have a survey because I knew about the problems. It went on to say that I had redecorated deliberately to hide these issues.

This was of course a worrying time, but my solicitor was clear that all the replies to enquiries during the sale process had made clear that the buyer must do their own checks on condition and if needed have a survey, and that I was clearly not qualified to give any opinions that could have been reasonably relied upon (I was 20 at the time!).

Thankfully, the matter was closed quickly and apart from a few quid in legal fees, it did not cost me any money.

There are two clear lessons from this story.

Firstly, unless you have considerable expertise, you should seek professional guidance on the structure and health or any property you are buying. Often vendors will decorate to show off a property, and there is always a risk that problems have been hidden. Literally 'papering over the cracks'.

Regardless of the ability to buy for cash and avoid a mortgage provider's survey conditions, any buyer should do basic investigations on the integrity of the property. I almost bought a property a few years later and took my father-in-law (a Chartered Surveyor) to a second viewing. He did a silly jump in the corner of the room, and after we left, we suggested an investigation into the floor. I paid for a carpet layer and carpenter to lift the floor to investigate and found serious damp problems and rotten floor bearers. £100 spent and a whole load of problems avoided (the buyer had to replace most of the downstairs floors).

The second lesson I learned was to not be too helpful with information. Whilst it didn't actually cost me any money, there was a real risk that I could have been liable for costs had I said things that turned out to be untrue. Communicate via lawyers so that there is a record of confirmations or information provided, and responsibility clearly assigned. When we are selling property there is always a temptation to "sell" it and talk up the good bits and talk down the bad bits. Making sure you comply with the law on what information must be disclosed and what is the buyer's responsibility to discover, is critical.

Unpredictable Planning

By Jackie Tomes

I had always believed that as long as you use a great planning consultant, then you shouldn't have too many issues dealing with planning. This unfortunately wasn't how things went down on my worst ever planning nightmare. Now to confirm, we were working with an extremely experienced and competent planning consultant on this project, but even so you can never underestimate the frustrating negligence and incompetence of your local authorities.

This project required a couple of different planning applications under both prior approval / permitted development (6-week turnaround from submission), and full planning (10-week turnaround from submission). I had anticipated that the full planning application might cause a delay as it may have detail that the planning officer wasn't happy with, and as such had allowed for a 4-week contingency to accommodate that delay before planning to start any of the works associated with that application. The permitted development elements however were, in the words of our planning consultant, "a sure thing".

The problems began when we contacted our planning consultant to check in on our first application. For this one the planning department were obligated to provide a ruling within 6-weeks from the date of submission or else it would be automatically granted, so as far as I was concerned this was therefore a legally binding deadline, with absolutely no chance it could be extended for any reason.

I couldn't have been more wrong!!

What I hadn't realised is that the planning department don't seem to have any obligation to look at the application and let you know if something isn't correct, and if it isn't 100% correct then their deadlines mean absolutely nothing. But surely nothing could be wrong with the application as I'd used a highly competent and respectable planning consultant?

After four weeks of the initial submission we phoned the planning department just to check everything was OK, and they couldn't find any record of the application in their system! It took two more weeks to find out what had happened. You see, we were applying for two flats above a shop to be made legal, and it turned out there were two different approaches we could have taken to make them legal, and we had chosen the wrong one!

We eventually found out that our application was sitting on a pile of paperwork on the wrong desk, being completely ignored, and by the time it was found it, it had put us right back to square one around the same time that we should have already received our permission. We were then told that our next application would be sped through the system due to the fact that no-one had picked up on this error and let us know. Of course, this didn't happen! We eventually received this first application back 21 weeks after initial submission, over three times longer than the expected 6-weeks.

However, the delays didn't stop there - we still had the full application to get through. For this one the planning officer wasn't happy with a couple of details such as the size of the dormer, or a bay window to the front façade. But instead of contacting us to discuss the details they weren't happy about within the 10-week timeframe, they just decided to wait until the very end of the deadline and just refuse the application. After some back and forth over various details, this application was eventually granted after 18 weeks.

But the saga didn't end there. I subsequently found that our draftsman had very kindly included various extra details within the drawings for the full application, such as what materials we intended to use on the cheeks of the dormer, and a stylistic line of red bricks to the front façade just underneath some new windows that were being put in. But as we all know, building works don't always go according to plan. We found that the windows actually needed to bisect the red line of bricks on the front façade due to internal ceiling heights, and we'd ended up using cladding on the dormer cheeks rather than render as was noted in the plans. Due to these tiny additions (alongside various other complications) we ended up having to make another planning application to make amendments to the plans which took another 12 weeks to fully resolve.

It turns out that even with experienced planning consultants and draftsmen on board, you can still have many, many issues when dealing with planning. The various planning applications for this project should have taken a total of about 14 weeks to get full approval, and they were all simple applications that should have had very few complications that could have extended this timeframe. However, they ended up taking about 32 weeks in total from the very first submission to when we finally had all permissions granted, on a project that was originally supposed to be fully completed within just 20 weeks! Not something anyone needs when working with expensive bridging finance.

The Bomb Map That Saved the Day

By Angelos Sanders

This is an interesting tale of a small comment I made that almost scuppered the entire deal.

The property in question was run down and built in approximately 1850. The seller had clearly not maintained the property and the tenants had amplified the neglect by making the property a whole lot worse. A bridging lender was required, as the scope of works were significant and everything was booked in. So far, so good and nothing unusual yet. I showed the surveyor around the property and we were both in agreement that it was in a very run-down condition. The survey came back and the lender was happy to lend. Off it went to the solicitors who performed their magic and just before we were due to complete the lender had to send out the surveyor again in order to ensure that everything was good to go.

The tenants in the property were not very agreeable and because the previous owner had not necessarily had a great relationship with them, they did not feel inclined to try and help the process and were refusing to allow access for the surveyor to make his pre-completion visit.

It took weeks of negotiating and persuasion with the tenants to finally book a date for the final survey to happen. The seller was getting more and more agitated as he believed perhaps something untoward was happening with the delays or that I was getting cold feet and wanted to pull out of the deal. He gave an ultimatum; complete by next Monday (it was Wednesday) or he would pull out of the deal. Credit to the estate agent as they tried their absolute utmost to persuade the tenants to allow access, which they finally did.

I met the surveyor on the Friday afternoon before the Monday deadline at the property and took him around again for a second visit to ensure that the lender was completely satisfied with everything, and everything seemed fine.

We stepped outside into the fresh air again and we were looking at the front of the building and I made a passing comment that it was the worst looking property on the street, which it clearly was. The surveyor then asked the question, why was it the worst property on the street? Was it simply neglect, or was it because it was rebuilt after some World War II bomb damage? Perhaps it had been rebuilt with mundic block (mundic block is something that lenders are not happy with, as it is a poor and unreliable building material.) I reminded the surveyor that on Monday we needed to complete otherwise the seller would pull out, so there was lots of pressure on me.

Monday morning arrived and the surveyor's report came back saying that there could be an issue with mundic block. Alarm bells started ringing because literally at the last minute this had been raised and I could potentially lose thousands of pounds in fees, and hundreds of hours of effort to purchase this property and all over this one comment. To make matters worse, the seller would in no way agree to a delay in completion.

I spoke to my broker and asked the question that if I could prove that it wasn't mundic, could we still complete today? A mundic block survey could take weeks and is quite intrusive and would no doubt cost more money and delay things considerably, so was a complete nonstarter. I racked my brains as to how we could prove it was not mundic without having to drill samples into the walls to be professionally tested due to apparent war damage. I then remembered that there was a comprehensive bomb survey report for the city mapping out where each bomb fell during World War II and if I could get my hands on it, I could then cross-reference it against the property I was buying and hopefully prove categorically that it wasn't hit during the war.

I raced down to the local library and found the map and printed a copy. I then opened up Google Maps, printed a copy of that area and highlighted where the property was located and then cross-referenced it against the bomb map. I found that the closest bomb had landed approximately 200 metres away, so out came my trusted green highlighter and I made it abundantly clear that this property was nowhere near any bomb strike, therefore not needing any reconstruction and hopefully it would be enough to reassure the surveyor that mundic block would not have been needed to be used to reconstruct the building.

The time was now approximately midday on completion day and everyone was feeling the pressure. I sent my findings to my broker who then forwarded it onto the underwriting team at the lender and I waited.

A couple of hours passed and I had a phone call from my broker saying that the lender would be happy to accept my findings that the property had not been struck in the war and that they were happy to continue lending in this project and we could complete today. What a relief!

The next time someone questions why we learn Geography or Map Reading or History at school, I will remind them of this tale.

I understand the surveyor was simply doing his job as he had to raise any potential issues with the lender, but luckily, I had a thorough bomb map of the city to fall back on for evidence, which helped save the day.

Surveyors vs. Builders

By Stuart Hallworth

The majority of purchasers do not appoint a surveyor to investigate the condition of properties that they buy. Some have a perception that a survey is a waste of money and contain too many caveats and so on. Furthermore, it's not in the estate agent's interest for a survey to be carried out, as they act for the buyer and are motivated to get the property sold for the best price, in the shortest timescale possible. A surveyor can and often does cause the buyer to back out of the purchase and the estate agent loses the sale.

If you are the purchaser though, wouldn't you want to be told about the things that can cost you money after purchase and damage your investment? If you're a cash buyer, you are all the more vulnerable to losing out financially if the house is hiding unforeseen and significant expenditure.

The surveyor is an expert who has been specifically trained to find defects in a building and report them to you as their client. When surveying an older house, I can usually find plenty of defects and issues that are not reflected in the price being paid. A purchaser armed with a report written by an independent surveyor is in a good position to renegotiate the purchase price or consider they may be better off buying an alternative property.

In the investment sector especially, some purchasers rely on their building contractor to check over the property. The builder is skilled in construction, but will they be able to carry out a survey of the whole property which is as good as a surveyor who has been specifically trained to do so? Does the builder have a working knowledge of issues that affect mortgage ability? Would they identify issues that are not to do with construction which still present a serious problem to the homeowner? Is the builder going to check the grounds and surroundings for legal irregularities and identify Japanese Knotweed at all times of the year?

Would you be surprised if I told you that I have inspected houses for mortgage purposes, being bought from building contractors in refurbished condition, yet have a feature that the mortgage lenders won't accept? I have even stipulated essential works to be carried out as part of a renovation but missed by the builder!

Chapter 4

Random Stories: 1

Buying Abroad

By Mark Homer

One of the single things that hurts new investors the most, and often financially nails them, is investing overseas.

It's not that property in any other country doesn't work for investment, it's the lack of local knowledge, the legal system, lack of control, lack of transparency, lack of contacts, and so on, but we can all be an expert or just as good, in our own local area.

You see, this can be a real minefield. There are so many companies offering dreams and it can all be very tempting. The marketing, the sun, the seascapes, the white flowing clothes on the beach and the dreamy lifestyle pictures all makes us think about being somewhere hot and idyllic.

There are also many real horror stories and even criminal investigations on selling, buying and owning overseas property. This should be a sign.

How many serious horror stories do you see from people buying local existing property? Little to none I believe. Certainly nowhere near as many because everything is far more transparent when it is local.

Comparables are easier to find and more provable and no celebrity is ever going to endorse some of the `minging' looking sheds (wooden fronted council properties) which can prove to be such good investments.

The main reasons people get into overseas property are:

1. They perceive that they can mix an investment with a holiday home (emotional decision)

Holiday homes and investment are not, in my experience, combinable.

It either works as an investment, or it is for personal use.

I buy watches for investment, and in the early days used to buy the watches I loved the look of.

They did not go up in value. The ones that go up in value do so for sound fundamental reasons such as scarcity of availability, heritage and provenance, demand vs. supply.

Some of them don't look great and would not be brands that I would choose, similar to houses in many ways.

2. They perceive the rental will be more of the year than it is.

Sure, you might be able to get 70% discounts from peak in Florida, but on what comparables? How much of the year will they rent for and what are the Homeowners association fees, property taxes, management etc.?

I could buy a Ferrari Testarossa for a few grand less than it is worth, but until you've owned one, you'll never truly appreciate how much they cost to run. Just because I bought it cheap doesn't mean it's a good investment because the clutch will still burn out every year, it will spend three months in the garage, and cost a lot of money in the first year in maintenance.

Most people think the be all and end all of successful property investing is discounts. It is not. The be all and end all is successful management, tenanting, and real net returns (which are more linked to management and tenanting than they are perceived discounts off made up valuations).

3. They believe it is the next 'hot-spot' (lack of experience)

Hot spot chasing is just the same as magpies chasing shiny objects. It is harder in the outset to master a local area and gain enough knowledge to reduce your risks than it is to take someone's word for something, endorsed by a celeb.

We bought five or six overseas, off plan new build properties in 2005 when we started and that was one of the biggest mistakes we made - we were green but keen - naive.

So what was this deal?

I bought an off-plan property in Bansko, Bulgaria.

The net annual loss after the mortgage, service charges and maintenance worked out an equivalent of €5,000 x 4 years = €20,000.

It was sold in March 2011 for €25,000 with a net loss of €50,000+.

And here was the sting in the tail:

The property only rented for three weeks in total. What looked like a great rental market with a nice income stream and cash flow turned into an absolute nightmare as lots of other apartments were built, which flooded the market.

Dishonest solicitors, rental agents, overpriced furniture packs didn't help either.

Word is that the developer has now evacuated from the building and - rack and ruin is on the horizon as there is no management company!

You see, we learned the hard way. We learned the expensive way. I tried to mix a holiday home with an investment. I paid too much for property I didn't understand which was outside my buying area for which there was a huge oversupply so would not rent.

4. They believe they can do it 'hands-off' (lack of experience/ emotional)

Overseas hands-off investing should be done with diligence. You should expect lower returns than if you became an expert yourself and weigh up the cost of not doing either.

It's not that the concept of investing in these countries that doesn't work, it's buying at arm's length. I know loads of Bulgarians who bought and did very well around the same time, but they weren't buying the new blocks!

Hands-off overseas 'investing' in my humble experience of watching this happen over seven years, is a double recipe for lack of control, massive voids, legal traps, huge issues gaining finance, and so on.

Shoddy House Purchase

By Jo Lines

The purchase did not go quickly – I had bought it directly from the vendor at the amazing sum of £29,000 – my car is worth more now! Trying to buy a house whilst having a baby was also a hurdle in itself. Having had my daughter prematurely at 32 weeks, I was in hospital for many weeks after she was born and even had my solicitor come to the ward for me to sign the contract paperwork.

Not really knowing much about property at the time and with very little sleep, I went about my first refurb project. Money was very tight and the property was a mess. Most of the work carried out was done by me, with the help of family and friends. We tidied up the kitchen and bathroom, redecorated and put new carpets in. Whilst lifting the carpets in the main bedroom to my surprise they had not used old newspaper but instead some very retro porn magazines, which made for some interesting reading!

Then came the windows. How had I not noticed these before? The frames were wooden and in poor state, I pushed on the window and it moved with my hand – to my shock the windows were made of plastic. There was no glass, they had been made out of Perspex! Until this day I have never seen anything quite like it. They all had to be replaced which had not been in my budget (note to self always check the windows), we also replaced the electrics, a family member who was an electrician who was kind enough to help but little did he know that the joists in the first-floor bathroom were rotten and he ended up putting his leg through the ceiling.

I owned this property for nearly two years and sold it at a very good time in 2001 effectively doubling the price I paid for it, so it wasn't all bad. A great learning curve and first steppingstone on the road to refurbishing properties.

Dog Viewing

By James Clarke

This would have been in late 1999/early 2000 when not much was selling and the majority of the stock on the books of the agency, I worked for at the time was multi-agency. There was a lot of available property on the market at this time.

As an 18-year-old I went out on a viewing with a couple to have a look around a bungalow in the city. I went into the bungalow and showed the couple around. They quite liked it. What I found strange was a dog was lying in its bed in the hallway. The dog looked up at me and then sat back in its bed. I thought this was odd as there was no mention of a dog on the viewing notes.

When I returned to the office, I spoke to my manager and he couldn't remember as it had been such a long time since we last did a viewing on that property and we thought it was empty.

I managed to get hold of the owner and he apologised as he had completed on this property the week before and forgot to tell us that he had sold it with one of the multi agents. So, in fact the dog belonged to the new owner who was now living there!

Probate and Cats

By Jo Lines

My career progressed quickly within the world of estate agency and before long I was out valuing properties. I worked for a busy corporate estate agency and would conduct 6-8 market appraisals per day. There is one story that springs to mind when you say 'property nightmares' and to this day it still gives me nightmares. I was very new to valuing and was about 23 years old. I was told in the morning meeting to pick up some keys from a local solicitor to carry out a probate valuation. I had no clue what probate meant but thought if it was just pick up keys and go to an empty property and take photos; I thought it would be a quick easy one for me.

When I got to the solicitors, I handed over my business card and asked for the keys to the property. The receptionist kindly handed them over and off I went; she had not given me any instructions or details, just the address, and as usual, a massive bunch of keys.

As I finally found the property, it was on a large estate with ridiculous numbering, I sat in the car outside. I got a call from the solicitors to say they had given me the wrong keys! It was a warm sunny day and I was literally booked in back-to-back with appointments. I told them I would return the keys by the end of the day and pick up the correct key so I could carry out the valuation but I would not have time to fit it in my diary that day now. As it was an empty property there seemed no rush to squeeze it in, so the appointment got moved to the following week. On the Monday I attended again, armed with the correct key, my camera, briefcase, and handbag. I got to the door and thankfully this time I had only been given one key so no faffing around trying to get in. I turned the key and as I opened the door, I was hit by the worst smell I had even come across. My eyes watered, my stomach churned – what on earth was it I thought? I closed the door and went back to the car. I rang my manager in the office. 'Is there a dead person in there?' I asked in dismay, nearly in tears. My manager rang the solicitors for me and confirmed that the owner had passed away in hospital and explained what probate meant to me.

She told me you have to go in and measure up and get the photos just go in and do it quickly. I took off my jacket and rolled it up to cover my face and attempted to enter again. As I walked in the smell was overwhelming, what was it? Where was it coming from? I went through the lounge to the back of the house, there was a massive very DIY type conservatory that was locked - I peered through the internal window into this room and I found the cause of the smell. I almost fainted, the devastation in front of me was horrifying.

The poor lady who had died in hospital had owned 12 cats who were now decomposing– they had all been kept in this conservatory and had obviously not had anyone to let them out or tend to them. I ran to the front door and promptly vomited. Those poor cats! It was a sight that will never leave me. Safe to say I left promptly and Rentokil were called in. What an awful situation, I worried that if I had gone in sooner when I first picked up the keys maybe this is not how it would have ended. I beat myself up and couldn't sleep that night. The following day I found out that the property had been empty for over three weeks since the old lady was taken into hospital. Not one person had been to her property or wondered what had happened to her beloved cats. She lived alone and after looking into things further she had nobody. The funds from the house sale were going to a local cats and dogs home – so sad, I just wish we could have done something sooner.

PART 2

REFURBISHMENT NIGHTMARES

Introduction

It is said that the road to disappointment is littered with unmet expectations. Frustration, anger, unhappiness, sadness and grief can all spring from this source. Refurbishments are prime examples of what happens when expectations and reality end up drifting continents apart.

Imagine this scenario: you have completed on the purchase of your property that you have spent months trying your best to purchase and all is well with the world.

You have the keys, you have the vision for how you want the refurbished property to look like when it is completed, and now you need to deliver the best refurb possible on the property. Unfortunately, when dealing with refurbs you are also dealing with many different tradespeople and all the dramas that are sometimes associated with them.

This is probably the most contentious section of the book because there are always three sides to a story; the contractor's side, the client's side, and then the truth, which is normally somewhere in between.

Occasionally the nightmare comes out of the blue, where the owner has not sought the necessary professional advice in order to unearth all the potential problems before beginning a project.

There are many factors that can cause distress when working on any project. The consequences of years of neglect can mean that a property may conceal severe underlying issues which are only discovered once work begins. For example, rotten floor joists, subsidence problems, common damp issues etc.

This section details some of these hidden problems so that you can be better forearmed and forewarned. With this better awareness, you and your contractors will have a better chance to identify any potential problems sooner rather than later. By not employing the right professionals and rushing to try and save time can often cost more time (and more money) in the long run.

Remember that common phrase, *'there's never time to do it properly, but always time to do it twice'.*

A common bone of contention is when tradespeople and their clients disagree on the scope of works and price. How many times has the smallest job been quoted for and was found to take twice as long and cost three times as much, compared with the original quote?

Of course if we bring in a 'professional' we expect them to price it right rather than have costs spiralling out of control. It is important that this matter is dealt with promptly and accountability given to the person who is in fact accountable. Then there is the case when the client changes the specifications or makes what, to them, are insignificant changes but has major knock-on effects with other trades. On top of all that there are the myriad of unforeseen circumstances that materially affect progress. There are times when there is a need to backtrack, undo and redo some work, which can obviously cause frustration.

In this section we will be sharing horror stories of builders who overextended themselves, procrastinating professionals, the many different issues that Building Control encounter, the importance of having a schedule and the perils of paying for work before it is complete, various issues building surveyors come across, what to be aware of when dealing with a listed building, and some ways to deal with refurbs and contractors to achieve a good outcome.

The stories in the Refurbishment Nightmares section cover:

- Building Control
- Refurbishment surveys
- Contractors and clients
- Another random assortment of stories

Chapter 5

Building Control

Quick Stories / Comments from Site

By Building Control

At attendance to home extension - cavity wall construction

Building Control Surveyor: “There’s a used disposable barbecue in your cavity (external cavity wall construction)”.

Builder: “Does that need to come out?”

At attendance to a home extension - roof felt

Building Control Surveyor: “I don’t recognise the felt you’ve used on the roof” (house extension)

Homeowner DIYer: “Oh it’s some spare garden weed barrier”

At attendance to flat conversions - sound insulation

Builder: “I ran out of sound (insulation) quilt for the floor so I’ve used expanding foam instead, is that ok?”

Building Control Surveyor: “Do you mean for small gaps?”

Builder: “No, for the whole of the flat”

At attendance to building conversion to flats - smoke alarms

Builder: "Yes all smoke alarms have now been fitted to all the flats"

Building Control Surveyor: "Have they been tested yet?"

Builder: "No I only finished off putting the batteries in last night"

Building Control Surveyor: "The back-up batteries? They're mains powered too, aren't they?"

Builder: "No just battery and I've used glue to stick them up on to the ceiling"

At attendance to an HMO - addition of bathrooms

Building Control Surveyor: "And where does the bathroom extractor fan terminate?"

Builder: "Into the cavity"

Building Control Surveyor: "You mean the ducting is through the cavity to outside?"

Builder: "No it's just the fan."

Building Control Surveyor: "So the steam is extracted into the cavity wall?"

Builder: "Yeah but that's fine because we have some holes at the bottom of the wall"

At attendance to renovation of existing flat - thermal upgrades to walls

Builder: "We've internally insulated the external walls with 50mm insulation"

Building Control Surveyor: "Ok, what product is it?"

Builder: "I don't know. I've used a mixture. I got some off Gumtree"

Building Control Surveyor: "Did the listing have a description?"

Builder: (On checking of the listing) "Yeah it says it's leftovers from a new kitchen, packaging good for insulation"

How to Get it Right: Localised Underpinning

By Building Control

A surveyor was alarmed when called out on site for an excavation inspection. Other than holding brickwork in position, the makeshift propping offered no real support to the corner and poorly fitted waste pipes and a rainwater pipe was leaking water into the excavation and saturating the supporting ground.

In reality, there were around five tonnes of load transferring through a timber prop that needed to be removed before the concrete could be placed. The excavation base had to be cleaned, widened and concrete poured as quickly as possible to minimise the possibility of settlement.

Fortunately the householder had a lucky escape, no thanks to the builder who could have caused serious damage to the property - albeit well intended. Underpinning should never be carried out without expert advice in bays wider than one metre and the bays should always be bonded together with reinforcement.

Undermining an existing structure requires careful consideration and planning to ensure that the loads carried continue to be fully supported and transferred back to the ground correctly.

The Association of Specialist Underpinning Contractors (ASUC) offer access, guidance and insurance backed guarantees to accredited members. It is an independent trade association originally formed by a number of leading contractors to promote professional and technical competence within the subsidence industry.

Beware of PU Foam Fillers

By Building Control

Polyurethane (PU) foam fillers - also known as 'fire foam' - are common in construction for fire stopping, but if you use them without properly understanding them, they can end up costing you money, creating worse fire risks and potentially ruin your hard-earned reputation.

Use of non-fire rated expanding foam is commonly used by DIYers to fix and fill holes and gaps in and about a home, but they are not an appropriate material for fire stopping. Furthermore, the propellant gas used to dispense the foam is highly flammable – if an ignition source is present at the time of application, the emitted gas can catch fire, potentially with explosive force.

Fire foam is usually tinted pink to distinguish it from other non-fire rated foams, but they're all different and have varying functions and properties - make sure you're using the right one. Without clear manufacturer's guidance, they shouldn't be used to fill large voids or openings as the foam's fire-stopping properties may only be effective and tested in narrow voids or gaps.

Some key points to remember about PU foam fillers:

- PU foams are combustible and generally will only offer fire-stopping properties when used in narrow voids or gaps.
- Fire foams are usually tinted pink to distinguish them from other foam products but they're not all the same - read the instructions.
- Most are only suitable where the gaps to be filled are 10-30mm wide, such as bed and side joints to lintels, frames and small penetrations in blockwork walls or concrete floors.

How to Get it Right: Roof Truss "Alterations" (Or Why Not to Cut Your Roof Trusses!)

By Building Control

Roof trusses offer a quick and efficient alternative to a conventional timber roof but they're quite delicate. They are structurally required to ensure that the timber chords and web sizes can be kept to a minimum and keep costs down. The central "W" shape is how most of the loads are distributed, so imagine the shock one of our building control surveyors had when he encountered this roof recently:

The owner had decided to carry out their own loft conversion for a bit more space and just removed the central web chords that were "getting in the way".

Once the web chords had been cut, the owners called in a builder in when they noticed cracking in the bedroom walls within days of the "alteration".

The roof tiles had to be taken off completely to allow the remedial work and the ceilings were propped down to the ground floor so that they could be retained in place while new trusses were inserted alongside and bolted to the trimmed roof members.

The buildings insurance providers refused the homeowner's claim leaving them with a very expensive repair bill and nothing to show for it.

When Means of Escape are Unacceptable

By Building Control

New build high-rise residential building

Builder: *"We don't want to provide an additional internal escape stair for the property, so we are wondering if we could provide a helicopter pad on the roof instead? Occupants could go to the roof and await rescue from there. From the fire service, or coast guard, or someone."*

In the Building Regulations guidance document Approved Document B fire safety, a means of escape is defined as *'a structural means whereby (in the event of fire) a safe route or routes is or are provided for persons to travel from any point in a building to a place of safety'.* Typically this is achieved by internal protected escape stairs, or in lower storeys escape windows.

It also defines what is not acceptable:

- Lifts (except for a suitably designed and installed evacuation lift);
- Portable ladders and throw-out ladders; and
- Manipulative apparatus and appliances, e.g. fold-down ladders, and chutes.

The reason is simple, a 'means of escape' route allows everyone to exit at the same time because they are permanent features. The three options listed in an emergency will need additional time to set up and will also limit the numbers who can use them safely at once potentially leaving people waiting behind at the route of the fire.

They also rely on someone having to do something for them to work and there are no continuing powers to ensure they are maintained and not vandalised, as such the expectation that they will always work in an emergency can't be guaranteed. It's one of the reasons why we no longer see hoses behind break glass containers in buildings; they have a limited life, rely on maintenance, and need someone to operate them properly.

Conversion to Flats Above a Ground Storey Commercial Use: Fire and Acoustic Performance

By Building Control

Fire resistance is pivotal when converting a building into flats. One of the most important design factors is compliance with fire regulations, especially fire separation of the units and the provision of a safe means of escape.

It is impossible in general to describe every requirement for fire and noise insulation, as there are many ways of achieving the required standards, and standards vary depending on the proposal. However, all conversions will be required to satisfy the Building Regulations. The regulations define conversion as a 'material change of use' and the whole or part of the building may need to be upgraded to make it comply with requirements, in particular means of fire warning and escape, fire resistance / protection, and sound insulation.

In general, separating (compartment) floors between flats and other storeys (above or below) must be upgraded to achieve one hour fire resistance and adequate sound insulation. This could involve the construction of an independent sound insulating ceiling beneath the floor or upgrading the existing ceiling. However, often with the conversion of a floor between an operating ground storey shop (or other commercial use) and a first storey flat, building work is completed from above so as not to disturb the use of the ground storey. A typical construction detail is to fix sound absorbent material between the existing floor joists supported between the joists with mesh or other, with a floating floor over on suitable resilient material.

Sound insulation is one of the most significant and expensive factors in converting a building into flats. It can be a complex science and it depends on a multitude of factors. In all cases it is important that the design incorporates the correct materials, and that the installation is carried out to meet very specific requirements and to the installation guidance.

It is essential that all floors are upgraded to meet sound insulation standards and there are various ways of achieving these standards. Advice on different methods are contained in Approved Document E – 'Resistance to the passage of sound'. There are also many approved systems by manufacturers – always check the 'Product Data Sheet' for demonstration of appropriate testing and certification of compliance to the Building Regulations.

Botching it up With Building Control

By Jackie Tomes

The next story is not here to undermine the story before (different city's Building Control), but to demonstrate that you as a homeowner/investor/builder etc. have a duty to ensure that you hold everyone involved in your project accountable, as even professionals can sometimes make mistakes. Ultimately, no matter how good your team is, it is down to you to ensure it all works.

I had always imagined that your local building control would understand exactly what you need to do in order to comply with all the relevant regulations. As long as you follow exactly what they tell you to do, that you should be fully covered on all counts of regulation such as structural safety, fire safety, acoustics, insulation, etc. However, it turns out that couldn't be further from the truth.

If you are unfortunate enough to have had a bad building control officer and only followed their advice, you may not even be able to pass some of the tests required to get a building control certificate for your works and that's if they can even be bothered to turn up to sign off your works in the first place! That's exactly what happened in our worst ever building control nightmare.

We (my builder and I) decided to just trust and follow our building control officer's advice and specifications to ensure that we would have no problems getting our building control certificate. This included detailed specifications on what we needed to do for fire protection/insulation, fire alarm systems, sound insulation, and thermal insulation. In fact, we just followed their advice on everything.

It wasn't until about three months into the project when we had already started finishing one of the flats that we brought around some more experienced developers to show them the project. During the tour they asked me what we'd done about sound proofing between the flats. Upon describing what our building control officer had specified, they looked very surprised and a little worried, which had me starting to feel a little worried! They gave me the number of their acoustic engineer and suggested I have a chat with him ASAP.

They had every reason to look worried. Turns out the building control officer had massively under spec'd what needed doing, and the acoustic engineer made it very clear that the measures we had taken had absolutely no chance of passing the acoustic tests that were required for new flats. The craziest thing was that we wouldn't even be able to get our building control certificate without these acoustic tests. So, by following the advice of the building control officer, we had made it impossible to get building control sign off! Even worse, had we found this out at the end of the project and then had to spend tens of thousands of pounds rectifying the error, building control would have had zero liability for their guidance!

As it was, this mistake cost us about £4,000 extra to rectify and added a further three weeks to the project as we had to install everything retrospectively and re-do various works that had already been completed.

But that wasn't the only thing we had been misadvised on. It turns out we had also installed the wrong fire alarm system too, meaning a whole new higher grade of system had to be retrospectively installed after all works had been completed in order for us to comply with fire safety regulations, costing us an additional £2,500.

Surprisingly, the biggest extra cost (and stress factor) came at the very end of the project once we'd finished all the works, completed all tests, complied with all regulations, and were ready and waiting for one more site visit from building control so that they could issue the completion certificate. At this point we were coming to the end of our 12-month bridge and needed building control sign off in order to refinance onto a lower interest long-term product. At this point we'd done everything we needed to do, so this should be simple, right?

Wrong! Building control went completely silent on us. They didn't answer emails, wouldn't return phone calls, wouldn't even allow me to visit them at their offices (first time I've ever been thrown out of the council offices by security!). For two whole months, I couldn't get a single response out of them. Eventually I escalated the issue with our local Councillor who escalated it with the head of building control, who finally arranged for the visit to happen.

In total the 2-month delay cost us around £5,000 in additional interest payments, making the final cost of choosing to work with, and following the advice of, our local building control an additional £11,500 on this project. Brilliant.

Chapter 6

Refurbishment Surveys

Grade II Listed Dream or Financial Nightmare?

By Lee Gough

I would like to share my experience of a Grade II listed building renovation. To give a little background, I have to say that I am reasonably experienced as I have bought and renovated well over a hundred properties. My story goes back to 2008 when I found a Grade II Manor House for sale that had been advertised in a trade journal with only a couple of lines and no picture. I had to see the property as it sounded intriguing and was in my local city. And wow I was not disappointed, a 13,000 sq. foot Manor House that was hidden, I could not believe that I had not seen the property before as it was in my own city and I drove by it every day.

The property had an application to have it demolished due to its poor state of repair, and for whatever reason this had not happened. The state of the building, most of which had not been touched since the early 1900s and what I can only describe it as having nearly every possible defect, from dry rot, wet rot, ceilings collapsing and roofs leaking, basically it looked like it should in a horror movie. We thought 'fantastic'!

My business partner and I at the time viewed it and fell in love with it and thought it would be criminal to have it demolished. We negotiated a price to purchase the property which we thought at the time was a 'bargain', just over £400,000. We were very excited as we wanted to bring a local historic building back to life and leave a legacy in the city, which we could be proud of.

On completion of the property, we had organised for a number of tradespeople to come, make safe and secure the property from vandals and stop it from further decay. At the same time, we invited the listed buildings officer around.

I can only describe that meeting as a heart wrenching and demoralising experience. I can still see him strutting in and walking past, virtually ignoring us. I still hear his words resonate, 'I want everyone to stop what they are doing, this is a listed building, and everything here is listed including the dust and if you're doing anything without listed building consent it is a criminal offence'!

Wait a minute, we have spent over £400,000 to save a building and invited you here and this is how you speak to us!

It was a very steep learning curve, as everything had to be approved by the listed building control officer. This was very frustrating as it slowed everything down.

To give an example, we wanted to move an outside garden wall. Normally this would have been a very straight forward and relatively inexpensive exercise. In order to do this we now had to get an architect to do plans and put a submission to the listed building officer. This was approved but it took six weeks. This application was granted with certain restrictions that needed to be adhered to. The wall had to be carefully dismantled, the original wall and the 'quoins' (the corner stones) needed to be reinstated in exactly the same way. We also had to source the original sand and where it came from, which was from a quarry miles away as we had to use lime mortar. We then employed stone masons who do not come cheap at £250 a day for each tradesman.

After a few more meetings with the listed building control officer, he could see that our intentions and the quality of work were being carried out to his specification. We then ended up forming a great relationship and he wanted us to work on other listed buildings.

By doing this project, we were able to find out the financial cost of buying and restoring a listed building, which are subject to strict controls on building work, are hard to predict and almost inevitably cost much more than those that apply to modern counterparts, which we were used to doing. Paying just over £400,000 for the building, we initially budgeted to spend between £200,000 to £250,000 to restore it. In the end these costs were far more than we could have imagined, coming in at over £650,000!

Taking on a listed building can be a rewarding experience for those who relish investing in or inhabiting part of the nation's historic fabric, but it is vital for buyers to go into a purchase with their eyes open when it comes to the costs of refurbishment, maintenance, materials, insurance, and energy use — or risk their fantasy residence becoming a house of financial pain, which we came to find out to our cost.

We also learnt from the project that listing does not mean a property's features have to be fixed in perpetuity. Conservation officers at local councils acknowledge that homes need modern bathrooms, kitchens, and heating systems if they are not to be abandoned in large numbers by their residents and left to ruin. I now understand that they are also required to ensure that inappropriate work is not carried out, and in so doing demand that owners carry out work in a particular way, using specific materials and techniques that can raise their costs significantly.

One of the biggest risks for buyers is to assume that the listed property they are purchasing automatically conforms to the listing rules. However, if any of the previous owners, sometimes going back in some cases as far as the 1950s, have carried out work incorrectly, it becomes the new buyer's responsibility to put it right.

Never has the saying 'buyer beware' been more appropriate.

In conclusion to my nightmare property, you may be asking would I do another listed building? In short, the answer is no.

Why, may you ask? My business partner and I learned so much about historic buildings, their construction, materials, and the workmanship but for us it is a business, and the process was too slow and bureaucratic. We don't regret the purchase as we formed a lasting business relationship that will be with us for a lifetime as we proved we could work together under mental and financial stress. We are both proud that we achieved our goal of leaving a legacy for future generations.

Building Movement - A Crack in a Wall

By James Barron

I was recently called to a house where an owner was becoming increasingly worried about a crack. The crack had been there for a while and the owner thought that it was getting worse.

The crack was between a house dating from around the 1930s and a 12-year-old extension. The owners had the extension built shortly after they purchased the house.

The crack was a full height crack between the house and the single storey rear extension. The crack was a tapering crack, becoming wider at the top than at the bottom. The crack was not major, being only about two millimetres wide at its widest part.

There were many possible causes.

The width of the crack was only one aspect. There is a British Standard setting out crack widths and severity and you would only normally get concerned about a crack over 5mm or so in many circumstances. But there are many different causes of cracking in buildings.

The important thing is that you must not jump to early conclusions.

It is equally important not to panic, but also not to ignore a crack. Because a crack has formed, the building is trying to tell you something and our job as surveyors is to try to discover what the building is telling us.

In order to consider a crack in a building and implications for ongoing movement, you have to have some knowledge and experience to understand the likely type of movement and the cause.

Let's consider the possibilities. The house was extended. It was likely to have a different foundation depth or type, or sometimes different ground conditions between the older and the younger parts. The younger part would almost certainly have a stronger foundation than the older, particularly if the older part was constructed before the 1960s when building regulations became commonplace.

Another aspect is the orientation and weathering of the building. The effect of sunlight and temperature can cause building materials to expand and contract, which can cause cracking and movement. This type of movement is not related to the ground or foundations.

The form of construction is also important. To understand the wall structure takes experience, because you can only normally see the inside and outside face and often don't have the ability to take core samples or drill tests. It's important to understand how the walls are built to be able to understand how they should behave in certain situations and what the cracking in the wall is trying to tell you. You can measure the thickness of the wall, the nature of the surfaces and look for clues in lofts or cellars to help understand how the wall is built.

For example, a lightweight concrete block wall, typically built in the 1980s and 1990s, will have a high thermal coefficient and be particularly vulnerable to thermal movement. Calcium silicate bricks are equally vulnerable and often have cracks formed because of the heating and cooling effect over a cycle of seasons. Modern buildings have movement joints incorporated within walls to help absorb that movement, but many older buildings do not have movement joints and will tend to form their own movement cracks. The important thing is being able to distinguish between a crack which has been caused without significant structural consequence and one which does have a consequence.

Rubble stone walls are commonplace in older buildings and particularly across the Southwest where there is a lot of building stone available. Those walls can suffer from compression of the rubble core within the thickness of the wall, which can cause bulging and cracking of the outward face.

Walls of single skin construction are very slender, sometimes only four inches thick. Understanding a single skin wall is important, as any cracking in a wall of that structure, no matter how narrow, could be a sign of structural instability particularly if built over single storey in height.

First you have to look at the crack.

How old is the crack? Is there dirt and debris within the crack or is it clean and fresh?

When was the crack last decorated? This can give you a good idea as to when the crack has formed or reopened since last filled and painted.

How wide is the crack? There are many devices that assist surveyors measuring a crack width and there are various 'tell-tale' devices that can be fitted over a crack to allow a period of monitoring over time.

What direction is the crack? Is it horizontal, vertical, diagonal or a mixture of all of the above?

Where is the crack in the wall? Is it around a weak point of the structure, such as around a window or door opening? Is the crack in the centre of a long panel of walling which is exposed to weathering and not provided with any expansion joints?

Also, does the crack exist on the inside of the wall as well as the outside? This is where knowledge of the form of wall construction is particularly important. A cavity wall is built with two layers of wall structure, separated with a cavity but still connected with wall ties. If the crack exists on the inside of the wall as well as outside, it will signify more likelihood of a structural problem affecting the wall as a whole. Thermal movement will more readily affect the exterior of a building as it heats and cools over a cycle of seasons, leaving the interior relatively unaffected.

What is the pattern of cracking? Is the cracking repetitive? For example, horizontal repetitive cracking in a wall might suggest a problem with the wall ties built within the thickness of the wall, such as wall tie corrosion. You wouldn't easily see this until the problem has become quite advanced.

There are ways in which a surveyor will be able to interpret a crack and read into it, to try and understand the source of movement.

The rule of thumb is the crack can usually tell you the line of movement. The movement is perpendicular to the crack.

For example, a horizontal crack in a wall, of uniform width, would suggest that the cause of movement is vertical, possibly expansion of wall ties causing a joint in bricks or blocks to separate.

A vertical crack in a wall, of uniform width, would suggest that the line of movement is horizontal. This could be some form of thermal movement where expansion and contraction within a panel of walling is causing a crack to form, often around a weak part, such as a window or door.

What the surveyor has to do is collect the data, consider the evidence and not jump to conclusions.

Turning back to the example in hand. This was a tapering crack, which was wider at the top than the bottom and existed between the extension and the original back wall of a pre-war house.

The crack was visible in the outside render between a cavity concrete block-built extension and a solid 9" thick brick original rear house wall. The crack was the full height of the single storey extension at this junction.

There might have been a crack on the inside wall, but this could not be seen. This was because there was a bathroom in this wall corner with the inside wall battened and boarded to give a service void for shower pipe work.

A small crack had formed between the tile grout in the corner which suggests that there has been some movement of the internal face of the wall as well.

For a tapering crack, what is the line of movement? I would suggest the movement is rotational. Because the crack is wider at the top and narrower at the bottom it suggests that the extension is trying to rotate away from the original building.

Following that line of movement, and the evidence collected, we should now look further afield than just the area where the crack has formed.

The extension was about four metres deep, which is typical for many single storey rear extensions built on properties. There was no sign of cracking in the rest of the extension walling - the only crack was where the extension meets the original building.

In the rear corner of the extension, approximately four metres away from the crack, there was a down pipe and storm water gully. There will be a storm drain leading away from this and to below ground drains serving the property. There was a manhole in the garden which could be lifted allowing some access into the drains.

The outcome

I recommended that the drains were surveyed with a camera inspection. This is a quick and simple, usually cost effective, operation which allows a surveyor to inspect the condition of the below ground drainpipes. What was found was a displaced pipe joint approximately half a metre from the gully. Water had been leaking out of the pipe and into the ground. Overtime, this washes out the foundation material and softens the ground. The building still exerts its pressure onto the ground, but being less able to resist those forces, the building slowly subsides. It was this downward movement in the rear corner around the down pipe, the rotational subsidence that had caused the crack to form. The pattern of cracking gave away the cause by pointing to where the source of the movement was.

Overtime, and without any remedial work, the building would continue to gradually subside until the crack became significant. Eventually, the distortion to the extension would have meant that it had to be demolished and rebuilt, at least in the affected area.

The outcome was that the homeowner made a claim under his household insurance policy. Most insurance policies will cover defects with below ground drains and any consequential damage to the building arising from those defects.

The broken length of storm water pipe was excavated and repaired.

Because the movement to the building was very slight and certainly not causing any structural instability, there was no need to demolish and rebuild or try and rectify the movement that had occurred. The cracks were professionally repaired including flexible jointing material and tie bar stitching across the crack.

As long as the source of water into the ground was rectified, the ground would stabilise and be perfectly capable of supporting the extension walling in the future.

The lessons:

It's very important not to ignore a crack, no matter how inconsequential it may seem. It's also important to look further than just the area of the cracking and to be able to read into the crack to try and understand what the building is trying to tell you.

Don't jump to early conclusions, but take the time to collect all the data, consider all the evidence and put all the pieces of the puzzle together.

Most importantly, don't panic! Most problems with buildings are repairable and as long as they are caught and rectified early enough and usually can be done with little disruption and cost.

Got a Void? Vent It!

By James Barron

There are some things that we learn at university that should never be forgotten!

I remember sitting in a lecture hall in the late 1980s, hearing a professor say the words 'got a void? Then vent it'. At that time, I didn't really understand the significance but the case study I want to share with you now will help explain what he meant.

A few years ago, I was asked to help with a situation being experienced by a homeowner. The owner had been at the property for around twenty years.

The problem was that the owner was discovering that part of a ground floor was rotting.

The situation was as follows.

The original house dated from around 1820 but had been heavily altered and extended as is typical for many properties. Around 20 years before it was purchased, an extension was built to house an indoor swimming pool shortly before the owner purchased the property, that pool had been filled in and the pool room converted into a living room with a bedroom and ensuite built within the rear part.

Within a few years of owning the property, the owner found that the floor in the middle of the room was beginning to rot and sink.

I should make it clear that the homeowner did have a full building inspection carried out before he purchased. Nothing was raised about the possibility of an infilled pool within the living room. I also want to make it clear that it was not my role to build any case against the surveyor concerned, but rather my job was to help put right the problems with the house.

This is arguably a good example of how homeowners can become dissatisfied with building surveys they have commissioned. It is very likely that there would have been nothing to put the surveyor 'on notice' of any problem with the floor. The swimming pool had been completely filled and floored over and, unless there had been some disclosure from the seller at the time, or some research on the planning history, there would have been nothing to give the surveyor any clue that there was a swimming pool there in the first place! That said, and with the benefit of hindsight, it was fairly obvious that there was a void under the living room floor. Walking around the floor, I could feel a hard concrete surface under foot to the room perimeter which then gave way to a much hollower sounding void within the middle of the room. This is easy to spot when you know what you are looking for, i.e. when the problem has become apparent. I like to make the point in matters such as this that, unless there is a trail of suspicion to follow, it is quite possible that something will become apparent during ownership of a house that simply was not apparent at the very limited time a surveyor was inspecting it for you.

Nevertheless, and needless to say, the homeowner was looking for some recompense for the problem they were experiencing and I'm sure the surveyor had some difficult questions to answer.

Turning back to the matter in hand.

The infilled swimming pool sat within the middle of a large room. The pool was surrounded by a concrete floor which would have been the perimeter of the pool area. By the time I was asked to have a look at the problem there had already been two small holes cut through the floor to undertake some initial inspection work.

To make things harder, the whole of the floor area was covered in a very expensive natural wood planking. Beneath the floor covering was an ordinary chipboard which covered the old pool area, supported on softwood timber joists pocketed into a ledge cut into the concrete perimeter and off a concrete block supporting wall built off the middle of the pool.

Through these small exposure holes it was obvious that the joists were rotten. The underside of the chipboard and the joists were covered with fungal growth which raised alarm bells about the possibility of a serious wood rot infestation.

Add to that the scale of the problem, the size of the pool was completely unknown, but my best guess from walking around the room and listening for where the solid concrete floor gave way to a hollow void, I estimated the pool to be around nine metres long by six metres wide.

To again complicate the problem, when the room was converted into a living room, it had been subdivided with a partition which now sat right across the area of the swimming pool. That partition had very expensive glass doors built within it and the usual radiators and electrical fittings, all of which were now well in the way of any remedial work.

Looking through the small holes that had been formed through the floor, it was obvious that the pool had been in-filled. The gap between the underside of the chipboard and the infill material was only about four inches, where visible. The problem was, of course, that there was no way of knowing how deep the swimming pool was. Assuming that the pool must be at least 1.2 meters deep, it would be reasonable to expect that there was something in the order of 50 cubic metres of infill material that might need to be removed. All in all, this was adding up to be a very alarming situation for the homeowner.

It was fairly obvious that the problem had been caused by a lack of ventilation to the void formed when the swimming pool was built over. Because the pool was surrounded by concrete, there was no easy way of getting ventilation into the void that was now formed. Although the pool had been filled in, a void had been left under the timber floor structure, sufficient to allow those timbers to rot and decay. This would have been an ongoing problem for many years, only becoming apparent when the floor started to sag and feel more uneven under foot, below the expensive wood planking.

Bear in mind that whilst all this was going on, the homeowner's living room was cleared of furniture and belongings to allow for a proper inspection. The bedroom at the back of the living room was out of use and the ensuite to that room was also unusable.

Turning now to the solution

It is never a good idea to leave any timberwork with fungal growth unattended as it can easily spread to other parts of the property. I decided to have a specialist timber and damp contractor inspect the woodwork to specify what needed to be done to the area around the infilled pool. Fortunately, that inspection showed that the infestation in the timberwork was a wet rot and that there was no sign of dry rot apparent. However, that advice was understandably qualified by a requirement to further inspect the area when the whole of the timber floor had been removed, exposing the infilled pool, and also when the skirting had been removed from the room perimeter and the stud work forming the partition was exposed. As I say, it is quite possible for wood infestation to spread to other parts than those areas which obviously show rot and decay.

In designing a solution there were two main things to consider.

First, that there could be no potential for future rotting and decay.

Secondly, that there would be appropriate ventilation formed to any void left under the floor within the infilled pool area.

You should note that it was impossible to tell whether the swimming pool was watertight. Obviously, there would have been some waterproof lining or tanking built into the pool when it was in use, but when this was decommissioned and in-filled with the brickwork and rubble material, it is reasonable to assume that those linings were punctured and, consequently, it was possible that water could be seeping into the old pool within the infill material. This would be an ongoing source of potential dampness and decay.

In order to overcome the problem, I designed a system of covering the old pool with concrete beams and blocks. These were designed to span from the original pool perimeter to the dividing wall which had been built to support the timber floor.

Thankfully, when the old floor was taken up and the pool exposed, all of the infill material looked to be inert brick and rubble. Presumably another building around the site had been demolished at the time the pool was decommissioned and the 'useful hole' in the ground was used to dispose of all the old material. I made sure that I had the infill material inspected by a timber and damp roofing contractor and a statement provided that it was suitable to remain in situ and did not need to be removed. This was a great relief to the homeowner as the cost of removing that quantity of infill, with the excavation being done by hand because it would have been impossible to bring a machine into the room, was exorbitant!

I also had the infill material excavated a little to ensure a void of at least half a metre between the underside of the new floor and the infill.

Ventilation was provided by channelling out through the concrete floor perimeter with a series of eight 'snorkel vents' raised upwards to outside air on two sides of the room. Unfortunately, it was only possible to obtain ventilation from two sides because of the way the room sat within the rest of the house. However, that did still allow a useful cross flow of air to flow through the void which remains below the infilled pool, helping to ventilate any dampness from the pool and infill material.

A new concrete screed was floated over the concrete beam and blocks and then the room could be reinstated.

That in itself was a complicated exercise requiring the reconstruction of a stud wall, careful reinstatement of glass doors, radiators, and electrics, together with a complete new natural wood plank floor covering.

All in all, the building work took about three months to complete. On top of that would have been around six months of investigation and planning, so the homeowners naturally experienced very significant disruption to their lives whilst all this was going on. All of this was a complete unforeseen by them as, when they purchased, they naturally assumed they had a fantastic living room to enjoy for as long as they wanted.

To this day I do not know whether their claim against the surveyor was successful.

The lesson:

Wherever there is a void in a building make sure that it is ventilated. This problem only occurred because the void beneath the covered over swimming pool floor did not have any ventilation and eventually, the timbers rotted out. Had ventilation been fitted, even with a timber covering structure, it is quite possible that rot would not have established itself and the problem would never have occurred. That might have meant that, to this day, the homeowners would never have known that they were watching TV over an old swimming pool.

The Nice, Refurbished Unmortgageable House

By Stuart Hallworth

Something that builders often don't bother about, but is regularly found in older houses, is a source of concern in the three most serious categories of defect – structural movement, timber decay and dampness.

About 20 years ago, I was inspecting a typical two up, two down type mid-terraced house for mortgage purposes. It was the type of property often bought by a first-time buyer. The vendor met me at the property and was a builder who had purchased the house, renovated it, and presented it back to the market. The property was in a good and modern condition and a credit to the builder.

On the rear side, it had a two-storey section extending out from the main house containing a kitchen at ground floor level and a bedroom above. Having practiced in this particular neighbourhood, I knew that it was common for the end wall of these rear sections to be of substandard construction, comprising of just one skin of bricks laid side to side, of 120mm (or thereabouts) in thickness. The correct standard is double this thickness. Upon measuring the wall, it was indeed single skin and being at both ground and first floor levels, the property did not provide acceptable lending security.

Tall walls of this type lack structural stability and they do not provide an adequate barrier against damp penetration. This increases the risk of serious decay to floors and other adjacent timbers on the inside.

How Dodgy can Dodgy 'DIY' be?

By Stuart Hallworth

Perhaps one of the most unbelievable spectacles I have encountered during an inspection for mortgage lending purposes was found at a property that had been created by the merger of two terraced houses into one single large dwelling. On the outside there wasn't anything to indicate that the two properties were now one, as the windows, two front doors and party chimney stack remained in position.

On the inside, the layout had been changed dramatically. Originally, each separate house had comprised a front reception room, rear reception room and kitchen addition at the back. Upstairs the layout would have been similar with front and rear bedrooms and a bathroom above the kitchen.

This merged property now had a huge front reception room spanning the full width of both former properties. The party wall and chimney breasts were completely gone. At first floor level, there were three bedrooms across the front in place of the original two. The ceiling in the middle room was sagging worse than I've ever seen a ceiling sag. There were gaps in the corners where the edges of the plasterboard had deflected upwards under the strain. The walls separating the rooms were lightweight partitioning with plasterboard dry lining. Then I remembered that the chimney stack was still in position, which would have been directly above the middle bedroom. Unfortunately, the roof space wasn't sufficiently accessible to assess whether all that heavy chimney masonry had been supported, but judging by what could be seen, there was a likelihood that it was supported over the two lightweight partition walls, which would not be of a load bearing standard!

It was the kind of situation where you realise the severity of the potential danger, you want to 'tip-toe' to the exit door as quickly as possible, in order to escape with your life!

This couldn't possibly be the work of a skilled building contractor and there wouldn't be any Building Regulation approval from the Local Authority. The fact that there was no sign of the merger of the two houses on the outside suggested the work was done on the quiet. One day I'll return to check if the house is still standing.

Home Cannabis Farms and Dangerous 'DIY'

By Stuart Hallworth

You always remember the strangest people and some of the strange things they say. When arriving at an ex-local authority semi-detached house on a Local Authority estate, I didn't expect to be met at the door by a housekeeper who said in a forthright and stern voice "you can't go into the loft". Back then, roof spaces were always inspected as part of an inspection for mortgage lending, although it was common not to be able to access it due to obstructed or blocked access hatches, but to be told at the outset that you can't go in there was unusual and suspicious.

I had been on the receiving end of such a comment once before, although on that occasion, the person at the property was the owner and spoke nervously. Upon arriving on the top floor, I found that the loft access hatch had gone and the whole of the ceiling in an integral cupboard was completely missing, allowing easy access. So I climbed up to see what the fuss was about. At a first glance all seemed fine, then suddenly I realised all the roof trusses were missing!

Trussed roof structures rely on the timbers spanning across the inner part of the frame for structural rigidity, but this also means that the roof space is obstructed by the timbers. At this house, someone had decided to make it more accessible by taking a saw to the trusses and cutting out the middle sections! There was a danger that the whole roof would collapse. Again, I found myself 'tip-toeing' out before disaster struck.

Getting back to the house with the housekeeper, a second much larger loft access had been created with a downward hinged hatch cover. It was padlocked. There were several cables running up and entering the loft around the locked hatch. What could they have been hiding?

Some years before that, I was inspecting a small mid-terraced house that had a long thin single storey section attached to the rear side containing a kitchen and bathroom with a small hallway in between. The occupant of the house was chopping vegetables in the kitchen. There was a loft hatch in the small hallway ceiling. I put up my ladders, climbed up, slid back the hatch, and turned on my torch. Through the gloom, the torchlight picked up leafy plants, cables and green coloured lightbulbs strung between the rafters. I reached down to my pocket for the camera, but the occupant was standing nearby, still chopping vegetables, so was assumed to be holding a knife! Was she aware that I had my head in the roof space? Surely, she was. She didn't say anything, so I decided the best course of action was to descend the ladders normally and not say anything either.

It is probable that the lady in that kitchen did not know there was a cannabis farm above her head. Maybe it was her partner's secret! More likely, it was the owner of the neighbouring house who owned the cannabis plants, as there wasn't a party wall separating the two houses.

Chapter 7

Contractors and Clients

Bungling Builders and Procrastinating Professionals

By Jackie Tomes

The most difficult thing with all builders and professionals is just trying to find the holy triad - good quality, reliable and affordable. Unfortunately, in the search for this you will inevitably end up working with some real duds, and the only thing you can do is try and engineer it so that the first time you use a new builder, trade or professional, it's on something small and less risky.

Which is exactly where I went wrong on our worst ever professional/trades nightmare!

I made the bad decision to try out a new structural engineer on an eight flat conversion project. They seemed brilliant! Nothing concerning was thrown up from the various due diligence I carried out, and if anything, they came through with flying colours.

The project got off to a great start, strip out was done within the expected timeframe and the structural engineer felt that overall not much would be required to ensure the works we were doing to convert this lovely old building would be satisfactory.

The problems began after about one month. We were once again putting in a dormer, and we were also removing some old wooden supports in the top floor to open it up for an open plan kitchen/lounge. It was my draftsman who first mentioned the floor joists to this top floor, asking me what our engineer had said about them as he wasn't sure they were adequate. Now the engineer hadn't mentioned them at all, so I quickly phoned up to get their thoughts and after a short discussion it was agreed that they'd better come back and have another look.

Now, originally this engineer had said that all we would need would be one steel beam in the top room to support the roof where we were adding the dormer. They then later decided that another might be sensible just to ensure that there was enough support where we were removing some wooden supports. By the end of the project, they had changed their mind and we had to replace the entire floor with new bigger joists and add four different steel beams to support both the roof and the new floor. That was four times as much steel as originally planned! But it didn't end there.

On one of his final visits our warranty surveyor asked us a simple question, what had we supported the steel beams on? You see, it looked to him like these massive steel beams had been supported on the chimney breast, and he wanted to make sure that they did in fact extend through to the party wall behind, because (as any building control officer or structural engineer knows) this type of chimney breast was not suitable to act as a primary support.

I confidently answered that of course the steels must be resting on the party wall behind. I could say this with confidence because:

- We had a fully qualified structural engineer plan and design it.
- They had been fabricated and installed by a steel fabrication company (who had been in this business doing this type of thing for the last 50 years).
- Our competent and experienced builder had helped to install them.
- The completed work had been viewed by our building control officer who hadn't mentioned anything amiss.
- We had a party wall agreement with the neighbour saying that we would be installing these in his wall.

Surely between these four experienced and competent professionals, there was no way that this had been done wrong, was there?

Turns out he was completely right, the steels had in fact been supported on the chimney breast rather than the party wall, and absolutely no-one had picked up on it.

The solution was not at all fun nor cheap.

We ended up having to install a nine-metre steel (costing over £5,000) along the ceiling of the floor below, which ran all the way from the front to the back of the building, with steel columns running up from that beam to support the steels above. The nine-metre steel had to be craned in through a 3rd floor window in three pieces, and the worst part was that we had already finished all works in the floor below, meaning that we had to make a massive mess and cut through new walls to fit the steel in and then make good again afterwards.

Needless to say, we did eventually fire the first structural engineer. It was a new engineer who came up with the final solution.

The result was approximately £25k in extra costs (made up of all the extra steel, extra install costs, cost to hire the crane, extra fees to design the steels, and then making good after all works), and about a 4-week delay to the project as other works couldn't continue until this was resolved.

Changing Suppliers Mid Project

By Adrian Wilkes

Going back to my very first refurbishment (a lovely 4-bedroom semi-detached house with a 120 foot+ garden), I learnt a very important lesson – not all shades of magnolia are the same!

The project had gone really well – the property was bought at a bargain price, and no real 'nasty' surprises were found during the renovations. All the walls had been skimmed, new kitchen and bathroom had gone in, new doors hung etc. and we were just waiting on the walls to be painted before the carpets could go down the next day. I was in London at these final stages but had called in a few favours to get the last room painted so that the carpet wasn't delayed, and the house would be ready for marketing photographs that weekend.

My parents were assisting in keeping the workforce happy – making cups of tea and dropping in food etc., another of their jobs was heading to B&Q for any supplies that were needed. We had run out of paint, so my father duly went off to the shop to buy some fresh supplies. He bought a big tub of Dulux magnolia and dropped it off, the guys finished the painting, and the carpet was laid the next day. It was not until checking that the carpet was OK, that we noticed that the dining room had two shades of magnolia which looked completely different! Instead of getting the correct variant of Dulux magnolia, he had bought another which the checkout guy had told him had better coverage, luckily it was just the one room that needed to be re-done.

Key lessons learnt:

- Don't chop and change products/suppliers.
- Whilst time is money, don't rush everything as it can end up costing you more in the long run.

Fighting For Plaster

By Angelos Sanders

During the Coronavirus lockdown in the UK, there was a massive shortage of plaster as the big manufacturers had ceased making it. As the weeks dragged on during the lockdown, plasterers across the country became more and more desperate for this precious resource. Forget fighting over toilet roll, bags of plaster were in massive demand, so much so in fact, that people were selling (and buying) single bags of plaster for over 10 times the usual price!

I was close to completing two refurbs and my plasterer needed this vital resource to complete the jobs. Patiently we waited for seven weeks and then a well-timed nod from a manager at a large hardware store gave me a call saying a big pallet load was scheduled for midday that day – exciting times and straight to action stations!

Off we set to purchase some plaster, the plasterer in his van and me in my car. As it was midday, it was lunchtime for most people and it seemed half the city had decided that the newly reopened KFC was the best place to go, therefore the traffic was bad (the hardware store and KFC were in the same area and shared the same route in).

I saw how the traffic was queuing and thought it will be best to skip the KFC traffic and filter in where the arrow said to merge, thus saving 20 minutes of queuing. Remember there was plaster to be had and there was no time to lose! As I was filtering in, I heard a knock on the passenger window from what I can only describe as a clearly rabid human being who was suffering badly from KFC withdrawal.

He was clearly upset that I was signalling to merge into the lane he was in as I had taken the initiative and not queued. I will not repeat the profanities and threats to my life and my car (though I am not sure why the Mercedes must suffer) and how my mum would soon be impregnated again (she is 71 years old and it would be a modern-day miracle, plus I am not sure he would be her type!).

My initial reaction was to face this person head on and defend the honour of the Mercedes, my mum and fillet him. But I thought if this ends up getting physical, the Police would be called by someone watching and that would delay or more than likely stop me from achieving my goal and that was buying the plaster to complete the refurbs, so I smiled, let him get it out of his system and he left.

I eventually drove into the hardware store and what do I see? Mr Angry Mother Impregnator (MAMI for short) was heading into the same store. What are the chances? He needed plaster too – perhaps it wasn't a lack of KFC but a lack of plaster that was driving his desperate behaviour?

I walked into the store and he was stocking up on bags of plaster and he saw me walking towards him. He looked at me and then looked down and looked up again. He started telling me that plaster was so rare and how lucky we both were to find some at this time. What happened to the same man who only five minutes ago wanted to become my stepfather? Gone was the angry person and "Mr I want to be your friend" had appeared and wanted to talk shop about plaster! I humoured him as he clearly had run out of puff from earlier and I enjoyed seeing this new sheepish version of him.

In the end, we both got the plaster we wanted, and I still only have one sibling… that I know of.

Digging 50 Tonnes of Rock by Hand

By Angelos Sanders

Sometimes there are times when you just have to get stuck in and start digging. This was one of those situations where there were no other solutions to the problem.

The house was a five-bedroom semi-detached property. At the rear it had a 40 metre long by 9-metre-wide garden, which had four tiers as it was on a steep hill. The previous owner had decided to extend the kitchen and had dug out the foundations and the surrounding soil and stone to make way for the kitchen, by dumping it up the garden forming a much steeper bank facing the rear of the property.

It was clear from inside that the property had not been loved for perhaps 20 years and that included the garden. In fact, upon viewing the garden when I was buying the property, I never managed to make it past halfway up the garden because it was so overgrown with dense shrubs and trees. One of the issues that was highlighted was the fact that the mud bank that the previous owner had created was touching the rear of the house effectively creating a bridge where damp was penetrating quite badly into the kitchen. There was no room for a small digger to excavate anything as there was no side or rear entrance and there were multiple thresholds and levels in the house, which would have mad access extremely difficult.

This project was going to be a flip, so I was going to buy it, completely refurb it and then sell it for a profit. I quickly realised that the garden was almost as big a project as the interior and so I started the garden work immediately. The first job was to clear the garden and see exactly what I was dealing with. I asked a few friends over a period of a weekend to join me in hacking back the shrubs and bushes. We even found three rotten sheds and we finally worked out exactly how far back this garden really went. It was huge, it was one mega long garden! It took four of us the entire weekend of hacking back to reveal the rear wall of the garden. It then dawned on me just how much work was needed to landscape this unforgotten but substantial parcel of land.

As the work continued inside, a few friends and I spent most evenings digging soil and rock by hand, to create an outdoor courtyard before walking up some block steps to the main garden. This would also stop the damp issue by removing the damp bridge to the house. This seemed like a great idea at the time and would definitely add value to the house, but I did not appreciate just how much was involved in creating this space.

Me and one or two other guys every evening, after a hard day's work, would swap our suits and change into digging clothes. We would dig the soil and rock with our pickaxes and shovels. The problem with digging shillet (a type of rock) is that once you dig it out, it becomes double the volume compared to when it was actually inside the hill. That was problem number one. Problem number two was actually getting rid of the soil and rock. There was a very narrow pathway between this property and the one next door, but it wasn't wide enough for a wheelbarrow to get through. There was no rear exit as the garden was surrounded by other gardens, so we couldn't remove it that way. We could have hired a helicopter, but unfortunately none of us knew where to hire a helicopter or pilot to pick up the tonnes of soil, which were very quickly piling up. The only way to remove soil and rock was to carry it through the house.

In theory, that seems like a simple thing to do. The issue I faced was that we had a PVC threshold at the back door, then we had to wheel it through the kitchen, through the lounge over another threshold, down a steep gradient into the porch where another threshold waited for us, then down three steps outside the front house where luckily, a friend of mine was able to take the soil and rock in his tipper truck to a local farm where it was used as backfill.

Fortunately, the digging took place during the summer months and we had lots of light and relative warmth to keep us going and were digging well into the late hours of every evening. I would often see neighbours poke their heads out the window to look out of curiosity, and sometimes with sympathy. With all of the digging we were doing; we became very efficient at removing the soil and stone. We had created a rally system going on where we would rotate diggers and wheelbarrow runners and lifters. A team would dig for several hours filling the two wheelbarrows that we had on rotation, and the running team with the lifters would lift the wheelbarrows over the thresholds and make sure that we didn't hit any obstacles on their way to the waiting tipper truck. It was very hard going, but with great music (best of 90s Pop), encouragement, lots of snacks, banter and pun competitions, over a period of two and half months later, we had managed to clear away about 50 tonnes worth of soil and rock.

We then had to create the footings for the retaining block wall and we had to dig some more. It is quite surprising how deep you need to dig for footings to ensure that you have enough for the concrete base ready for the block work.

After all the digging (we could have given Arnold Schwarzenegger a run for his money with the muscles we grew from all that digging) we finally did it! We had cleared the whole area, built the retaining wall, and built the blockwork steps leading up to the main garden. I was very proud of my team. We had broken this little mountain!

As mentioned earlier, works had to progress inside at the same time as the monumental task of landscaping was happening. Even up to the last few days before the house was going on the market, the inside was being painted and glossed with wheelbarrows of soil and rocks being transported through the house to be removed and taken away at the front.

Every morning, I would speak with my team and ask them to be very careful when moving the wheelbarrows through the house to avoid getting soil or dust on the wet gloss. Then what happened? I was glossing some skirting in the downstairs living room and one of the workers needed a hand with the wheelbarrow as it was quite heavy with soil. I said, "leave it with me, I will take this to the front." As I was pushing it past the kitchen and into the lounge, what I can only describe as a momentary lapse in concentration, I spilt the entire contents of the wheelbarrow all over the wet gloss. I will leave it up to your imagination as to what the first words that came out of my mouth were. Needless to say, I picked up the contents of the wheelbarrow, dumped it onto the truck, then salvaged the gloss situation, with my workers reminding me to be more careful in future with the funniest of sarcastic tones.

The garden was raked and levelled by hand in preparation for grass seeding. One thing I have learnt with seeding is that it usually takes about three times what it says on the packet to actually achieve a good consistent level of grass without patches. I was very pleased to switch from digging to watering every evening to ensure the seeds had enough water so that they would grow.

I'm very pleased to say that after all the efforts we as a team had put into this project, the property sold quickly and broke the ceiling price on the street for many years due to the high level of finish at the property, both internally and externally, which included the monster garden.

Always Trust Your Gut Instinct – A Mini Noah Flood Event

By Angelos Sanders

What is the old saying? Always trust your gut. Well, I chose to ignore it and it cost me. Early on in my investing career, I bought a project that seemed simple enough and that was to refurb an old house with a huge garage. The plan was to convert the large garage into a bedroom with ensuite. Planning was granted and the builder and I had a final walk around to make sure he understood the plans fully. The garage was made of block work and there had been some evidence of historic water staining at some point. I queried this with the builder and because it was a hot dry summer plus, he played on the fact that it would overrun on budget, he did not think that water-proofing tanking would be required. My gut told me that tanking the walls was a wise precaution, but as the budget was already tight and I had less experience in those days, I unfortunately listened to him and the build proceeded.

The refurb completed with few dramas and the first tenants arrived in September. What was a very dry summer, was followed by a very wet November and December. Just before Christmas, the tenant who was living in the room inside the garage conversion rang me up and said there was a slight issue with damp. The usual thoughts went through my mind was it damp or was it condensation? I arranged to go down and have a look to see exactly what the problem was.

I turned the key in the door and the water rushed out; it was as high as my ankle. My heart sank when I quickly realised the entire living area and bathroom was sodden. I quickly went into detective mode to see exactly what the source of the water leak. Was it a broken pipe? Was it coming through the roof? Or were the taps left on? The water seemed to be originating from the corner of the garage where there had been water staining previously. I ripped off the plaster-board and insulation to see what was going on.

The walls were dripping wet and the floor had a little stream running through it. I knocked on the neighbour's door to see if I could get their permission to have a look on the other side of the block wall. They kindly let me in and on the other side of the block wall was their garden which had a slope down through their garden into the block work where the garage wall was. Therefore, any rainwater in the concreted garden was running straight into the garage and straight through into the tenants living area.

After working out what the problem was and cursing myself for not listening to my gut, I realised the only solution to this problem was to prevent the water coming in in the first place and also make sure that should any water come through the walls, it would be stopped and controlled with a damp-proof solution so the living areas would never get wet again. I take pride in the finish of my work and to rip apart the expensive bathroom suites and all the walls, the insulation, the carpets and all the high-end furniture, was heart breaking, but it had to be done and it had to be done during Christmas and before the tenant returned early in the New Year.

It was back into refurb mode for me that Christmas. I pulled in my team and we tore apart the old water damaged items and stud work and completely cleared down the entire garage. We began implementing the damp control measures to ensure this problem would not happen again. Sure enough, despite long drying times with the tanking solution onto a wet surface and with the cold rainy season, works completed to schedule and no one would ever have known that Noah and his Ark were almost needed to be brought out of retirement. The tenant was very understanding and was very pleased to see his new (again) room ready for him when he returned in January. So dear reader, I would always say if in doubt get another professional opinion, but if you really know and your gut tells you that you should do something, it is usually best to listen to it otherwise you might end up paying twice.

Builders Overextended with a New Build

By Dave Ottley

Scenario C

- One of our regular clients had progressed from successfully completing many light and heavy refurbishment projects and had moved onto an ambitious new project to build six new houses, on some land that they had acquired and obtained the relevant planning permissions for.
- They worked with us to achieve a suitable Development Finance package of funding via a High Street Bank and proceeded to make a start on this new project.
- They were using the same building company that they had worked with for the past five years or so and had set a 12 month build cycle for the project.
- The intention was for the properties to be sold on completion and the total loan to be completed within 18 months to full repayment.
- The agreed loan was to be drawn down in tranches, following assessment of the completed works.

Almost immediately after initial groundworks had commenced, the project came to a halt as it transpired that their builders had over committed their existing workloads and had another project to finish.

This was totally out of the blue and whilst their builders were extremely apologetic, upon extended due diligence, all parties became aware that they were also in financial difficulty and would in fact be unable to complete the project at all. Our clients worked tirelessly to source an alternative builder and this time undertook extended due diligence, eventually appointing another builder, who could start the project five months later.

We returned to the bank and updated them on the unwelcome news of an extended project delay and cost overrun as the replacement builders also highlighted some cost "oversights" in the previous schedule of works. Fortunately, the funding bank remained supportive and after several weeks of re-negotiation, we were able to get the loan re-sanctioned at a higher amount and extended loan term, with the caveat of far more regular visits from their bank appointed Project Monitor, throughout the process of the build cycle.

This delayed build dramatically reduced the development profit for our clients and some 20 months later, the project was completed, with all six properties being sold and the bank repaid.

Points for consideration:

- Carry out extended due diligence on all the parties that are assisting you with development/investment projects, each and every time you undertake a new project.
- Whilst loyalty is an admirable quality, sometimes you need to work with new partners who are experienced in more challenging and difficult scenarios.
- As we all progress though our property careers, we can develop at differing rates to our advisors and sometimes need more expert help.
- Without this, it can cost you dearly in terms of profit on a deal and in this case study, the profit levels were reduced by nearly 90%, due to increased building costs, project monitor fees etc.
- Be mindful of stepping out of your comfort zone. Whilst we all like to improve our knowledge and "step up" to a new challenge, sometimes it can be more profitable and rewarding personally to "stick to what you are successful at".

Preparing Schedules and Paying For Work Before it is Complete

By Dan Anson-Hart

We have learnt a lot over our first year in property and mainly at either our own expense or from hearing about the mistakes of other more experienced investors. This is a huge reason why we are so excited for this book to become available. There is so much value in learning from other people's mistakes. There is no better way of avoiding mistakes than by learning from others that have already trodden on the same path we are heading.

We started out in property using the Rent-to-Rent HMO strategy in order to build cash flow to allow my wife Jodie and I to leave our day jobs in teaching and sales respectively.

Now out of the day jobs, we are working to build long term wealth by purchasing assets and working to build a portfolio with as many doors as we can. During my spare time, I like to improve my knowledge with personal development, either via podcasts, audible books, or phone calls to trusted and more experienced investors/mentors like Angelos Sanders.

We began taking action and founded our first property company, Your Trusted Tenant. 12 months on, we have secured two purchase lease option HMOs and three Rent-to-Rent HMOs totalling 25 units/ tenants. This has meant that Jodie no longer has to teach and can now spend her time helping me manage our property business whilst continuing to be an amazing mum and wife to me and our children.

Putting my teaching background and passion for property together has helped me transition and become the host of a property networking event in Cornwall alongside Angelos, the Professional Investment Group (aka PIG – www.pig.network) Cornwall. This in itself has opened up so many new opportunities at a time when I "didn't have the time" but just said "yes" to every opportunity that came to me.

All of this has been achieved whilst in full time employment and with a young very busy family. I'm not saying this to brag but hopefully to help motivate you. This has been anything but easy, but with a strong "why", good education and a great support network, you can do this too!

We were on our fifth refurbishment property with the same builders/property maintenance team we used on the previous projects. We may have become a bit too comfortable a bit too soon and had ended up having a few teething issues on this final refurb together.

The standard procedure to obtain quotes was simple, we walked around the property together and discuss what work is needed to be carried out. I would then follow this up with a detailed schedule of works to confirm what was discussed.

The building firm we used was a relatively new start up business.

What we found on this most recent property refurbishment was that we began to get too comfortable with the team and perhaps we didn't give as detailed of a schedule of works as we had done previously. The refurb was the exact same as three or the other four projects recently completed and the only differences were that there was an external door in the kitchen to be blocked up and an internal opening/serving hatch from the kitchen to the conservatory to be opened and widened to make a walk through.

The agreement with the quotation for this works, as we understand and interpreted, was that this work was all in the price and quoted for. The contractor had been to visit the job and had seen and understood the work needing to be completed. I also sent a video walk through explaining all of the work and sent this across to them also so they had this as a reference when quoting for the work.

However, the first issue came when they quickly realised that the opening they were taking out and widening was not in fact a stud wall as it had sounded when we inspected it (it sounded hollow when tapping or knocking on the wall) on our initial walk around but it was in fact a brick/stone wall. With this in mind, we were now a little more concerned about the structural stability of the opening and as a result more work was needed to be carried out than the builders had originally foreseen.

For this reason the builders said they would be charging us more than we originally agreed for the work as they would need to do far more structural work than they originally expected and quoted for. My argument here was that they had quoted for and given me a price for the works having walked around and seen the project and to then start adding further cost to the works halfway through was a little unfair. Arguably yes, there is going to be more work required than originally anticipated, however I also have the stance that they should have budgeted this into their original quote as the "experienced builders".

The extra work they were now needing to carry out was to build two supporting block 'pillars/supports' either side of the opening to support the lintel above just to be safe. Rather than just make good the scarred opening, they wanted to charge an additional £2,500 for this work which I was not happy about personally. In my head they had seen the job that needed to be carried out. They knew what the wall/house looked and sounded like when tapped and felt it unfair to then add an additional £2,500 onto the job because they hadn't been thorough on their initial inspection and walk around. This became a sticking point as I am sure you can imagine.

I therefore called for a team meeting to discuss all of this with them and expressed our frustrations at this additional charge. We then came to the agreement that we were perhaps both at fault here in that I perhaps wasn't clear enough on our schedule that there was the possibility that the wall could be more solid than first thought. I believed that they should have either budgeted for the wall to be a bigger job than it looked and they should have built in contingency or at least in the quote mentioned that it was based on the opening being a stud wall but if it was more substantial, then they would need to reassess the price. We would have then been far clearer with where we stood and happy to accept the possibility of increased costs depending on different scenarios.

We have definitely now learnt we need to ensure a written contract is in place between ourselves and our builders and that a very detailed and thorough schedule of works is in place before all work is to begin so that all eventualities are planned and budgeted for.

Another issue we experienced and was the final straw for us with regards to continuing to work with this team, was that with the above concerns and conflict we had regarding the increased charge and work for the opening. The builders insisted that we pay the final payment before the work was completed. I naively agreed in order to help keep peace, however this has now come to bite me in the arse as we paid the final instalment back in early 2019 and in 2020, we were still waiting for the work to be completed to a high standard.

This delayed completion of the already paid work is becoming very frustrating and the fact that they have now been paid means that they were not very motivated to complete the work. Don't get me wrong, I did trust that the work would get done, however I am very disappointed now in myself for paying before it was and for just how long it took them to pull their finger out and get it completed.

All in all, this project has taught us, and by hopefully sharing the above, has also helped you with future refurbishments.

- Ensure you have a written and signed agreement or contract outlining what work has been quoted for and what happens when further unforeseen eventualities or extra work comes up on site.
- Have in this contract an agreed payment plan, ensuring that you do not pay for the full amount of work to be completed until you have snagged the project and the work completed and are happy.
- All this has also taught us to ensure we have an agreed deadline for the work to be completed in order to keep the builders accountable and on track.
- I hope that this has helped open your eyes to the importance of having detailed contracts in place and not to pay for work that has not yet been completed and snagged.

Being a Builder isn't Always Easy

By Mike O'Shea

Being a builder is great. It's fun, rewarding, challenging, and satisfying. Being able to bring a client's dreams into reality is the best part. It can also be stressful, tiring and draining. Our company has been helping clients with their projects for many years and we have had great times and some not-so-great times.

I very occasionally look back at the time we set our company up and question whether we chose the right moment to begin our journey. We have been through the largest global pandemic the world has seen, faced product shortages that have been unprecedented and seen cost rises that have been eye watering. With or without these challenges, we wouldn't have been able to get to the point where we are now if we hadn't taken the plunge.

We have completed some great projects over this time and we have had some difficult projects as well. The greatest challenges faced by our company and those that caused the biggest nightmares were people, staff and contractors, clients and suppliers.

Staff and contractors

These are some of the biggest challenges our company faces daily. Following the pandemic, and I can only assume that because people were spending more time at home seeing work that needed to be done and this has helped the construction industry to boom. This has made it virtually impossible to find good trades people who aren't booked up for a decade in advance. You can find poor tradespeople very easily, but of course, no one wants a bad job done.

Poor tradespeople bring their own nightmares. We have seen plumbers who say they are plumbers but should be called water feature installers. We have seen plasterers who say they are plasterers but should be called artexers. The nightmare faced by contractors like us is that we can only take someone's work and experience on their say so. It is only when they have started work that you realise your mistake. By then, it's too late and is costing money.

Getting self-employed contractors to turn up on site is another issue and some of the excuses we have heard for not turning up are mind boggling. This year alone, we have had someone not come in as their "pet reptile had an asthma attack" (can reptiles have asthma attacks?), "I've caught a very bad virus" (but was in the pub the night before) and "I've been arrested" (that's the 7th time in a fortnight, maybe you should think about staying in at night!). We have around eight full time contractors and use more on an ad hoc basis and it is still not enough to satisfy the work load we have currently.

Clients

We have had the opportunity to complete some beautiful projects for a range of clients in our tenure. From a small bathroom refurbishment through to a full house refurbishment overlooking the beach and sea. The projects have been varied. We have also had some awful projects to deal with.

One of the biggest challenges is the client's understanding of the project and what's involved. Some clients don't realise that you require planning permission to build a new property from scratch (honestly), which in turn has caused delays and headaches. We are a very flexible company and have helped clients to obtain this but this causes delays and confusion, which our company seem to have borne the brunt of.

We are a reputable company who provide high quality workmanship. Some of our previous clients may not really like this concept and they are the ones who would be happy for us to cut corners, which is something we will certainly not do. Some think it would be OK to carry out works without a Party Wall Agreement, or just use the original wet plasterboard for new tiles, and to "just fill over the hole where the dead rats were found"!

On the whole, our clients are fantastic and our contractors provide high quality work. We have faced a few nightmares along the way and can imagine that we may face a few more in the future. Would we want to be doing anything else? Absolutely not.

Subsidence Problem

By Ian George

We bought an end terrace buy to let property as an investment in 2008, right before the crash. It was all running smoothly until we decided to re-render the gable end of the terrace because there was a bit of damp coming in and the tenants were complaining.

About two days into the job the builder called me up and said I should come and see what he'd found.

Between the main building and the tenement there was a crack two inches wide the full height of the building. It had been stuffed with newspaper and re-rendered over the top to cover up the crack. There was no evidence externally or internally. The previous sellers had done a very good job of covering it up.

We contacted our insurers but because we had changed insurers that year, they said that the previous insurance company was most likely to be liable so we spent the first six months arguing between the two insurance companies over who was responsible for covering our property.

After that was decided, the Loss Adjuster said that he thought the subsidence was due to drainage so we had to repair the path, and then monitor the movement with crack gauges for 18 months.

18 months later and there was still a small amount of movement, so the next stage was to get some trial pits and boreholes dug to see what was underneath the foundations. What they found was old power station waste material and a bedstead made from iron. The Loss Adjuster argued that because the bedstead had corroded, the ground below had settled and that's what had formed the cracks.

He claimed that as it formed part of the original construction, the insurance company was not liable.

Fortunately as a civil engineer and with a structural engineer acting on my behalf, we argued that the corroded steel would only let the foundations drop by a couple of millimetres and there was no way that those cracks could have been formed by a settlement of that small amount.

Thereafter ensued three years of back and forth with the Loss Adjuster trying to come to some form of agreement. At one stage they offered us £15,000 to go away and to settle the claim. I ended up having to record our conversations because he kept on changing his mind.

Eventually they agreed to an underpinning solution along the gable end but the structural engineer pointed out that if they made a hard point of the foundations there then it would make a hard point along the whole terrace so the whole terrace would have to be underpinned - some 20 houses!

After that I suggested to the insurance company that we put the property on the open market declaring the subsidence and the size of the cracks and that they compensate me for the difference between the sale price and the open market value had the property not been damaged. So that is what we did.

Luckily, a builder took on the project, we sold the property and it has now been sold again hopefully declaring the cracks and the subsidence. This important lesson means we will never take on a property that shows signs of subsidence again.

Procurement and Contract – Selection of Contractor and How it all Panned Out

By Richard Mitchell

Procurement which method to use?

Methods of procurement for any project are critical to the outcome.

For those not familiar with project costing and tendering there are many different types of tender and form of contract. Ultimately you are effectively being asked to decide on the optimum route to completion of the project before you have all the information.

With almost 40 years of experience in the construction industry I have been lucky enough to work as a contractor, client, and consultant; this gives me a unique insight into the options and benefits of the various methods.

This is about nightmares, so I will stick to what was selected and explain how this proved to be a prudent decision.

The first thing you need to consider is whether you have the experience to manage the commercial aspects of the project and contractual obligations.

In this instance, despite having worked as a commercial director in the Middle East I decided that to run the design and project management and do the commercial aspects of the project, which would be challenging and this combined with the requirement for a Royal Institute of Chartered Surveyors (RICS) accredited surveyor being appointed by the bank related to the development finance, it made sense to have a professional Quantity Surveyor (QS) on board.

Early stages of the Commercials

To step back a stage, the first thing that you need is a budget and this needs to be based on as many facts as possible and some assumptions, budgets are a moving target and with refurbishment projects of age; there will always be unforeseen circumstances. In order to establish the budget, you need to have a project plan, understand where you are heading and what you plan to do, it will more than likely change: Prepare a cost plan of major costs so that you can manage the changes.

I prepared drawings based on an assumed scope and layout, having personally done a tape measure survey of the property and prepared the drawings, (beware old buildings are not square!) I employed an architectural technician to do an accurate survey and prepare existing plans and layouts based on my preliminary drawings. This turned out to be prudent as the layouts needed to be tweaked and this gave a fully accurate basis on which to base quantities for the Bills of Quantities (BOQ).

I applied for pre-app (planning advice prior to submission of a formal planning application). I got a positive response. This was one of the requirements needed to be able to present to potential investors and to approach the bank for development finance.

I also had a third-party company interested in taking over the property. They priced the work, I priced it. I had the selected QS do an estimate and paid an RICS surveyor to do a Red Book survey and valuation and to include projected GDV returns. These were used to take to the bank and provide further evidence of the credibility of the scheme.

For information I ensured the RICS surveyor was on the panel of surveyors used by the bank providing finance and that the QS was RICS qualified and would be approved by the bank for appointment to do reports and valuations during the project. This saved me two additional fees. So, if you can use this on your projects it could save you thousands of pounds. It is possible to do a dual appointment for the QS to act for you under the contract and to report to the bank but get pre-approval. Incidentally, we did not agree with the Red Book Valuers GDV and by talking him through the USPs of the project and providing evidence-based comparisons, he lifted the value in an addendum, which helped with the finance.

After the initial pre-app, we immediately applied for planning. Please bear in mind that all of these activities have cost implications and you need to ensure that you have access to the funds you need to get the project to a stage where you can get finance and investors will be willing to look at this. In my case I used bridging finance. The planning was successful (not without its challenges, that was a separate nightmare!). Once planning was in place, funds were released by the bank as there was a planning gain, lifting the project value to bring it into line with the Red book valuation.

Delivery strategy

We decided to do a phased approach to the project and have an enabling package prior to the main works. This was risky as it meant ripping out the internals to expose the structure. There was risk, as if we could not then do the work as planned, we were committed, and certain other options had to be ruled out or would have cost significantly more to implement. The enabling package was tendered and won in a lump sum competitive bid, to rip out and clear the site. This was done successfully and completed to program and within budget.

Thank goodness we did the enabling package, with the structure exposed, whilst the layouts only needed to be tweaked, the methods of construction changed, due to extensive alterations to the original building that was built in the 1700s. We had brick, block, cob, timber frame and stone walls. We could then accurately measure what we could reuse and what would need to be done to complete the work. Structural calculations and building control drawings could be prepared representing exactly what we would build. We discovered several issues that would prove to be a challenge.

Procurement method

I discussed with the QS what I wanted, which was to try to work in a collaborative way with the contractors. I went through a Rolls Royce prequalification process for the contractors all confirming their interest to quote. Four contractors were selected and tendered. We decided not to do a lump sum contract, my experience told me that with this type of project there were always surprises, despite our best efforts to identify any potential issues pre-tender. Thank goodness we did! We built in additional quantities to the BOQ that we could use as a contingency, this was mainly on the advice of the QS, who needs to take credit for this. We selected the JCT form of contract with contractor design for certain elements of specialist work. We also prepared a very comprehensive schedule of rates that covered any possible change and day work rates, this covered us for any works not priced by the contractor to ensure they were tied into rates.

To clarify we went for a re-measurable contract and not the usual lump sum with variations, this proved to be the single best decision we took. With a re-measurable contract, the contractor does not have to price in risk to the same extent as with a lump sum contract, so you get actual rates for the work.

In the end we all got the pre-tender estimates wrong! Pricing is a black art, it is driven by many factors beyond your control, so no matter how good your information, the tenders returned will not necessarily be what you are expecting. Our pre-tender estimates were between £500,000 and £545,000 across four assessments. One company declined the tender during the tender period as they had a full order book and the three remaining tenders came in way over budget, with the lowest being circa £800,000. (Highest over £900,000). Our initial thought was to panic, we had a stripped outbuilding and a price that made the returns very sparse, far too close to go ahead. By this stage we had 11 investors on board, who had put in £300,000 and bank finance secured, but not enough to get us to the end based on these tenders.

Post tender analysis and actions

The QS and I sat after he had done a thorough tender report and there was only one contractor who we could negotiate with. We went through the project from start to finish. It was decided that I would redesign the project to effect savings. We now knew the building inside out and by changing layouts but keeping the overall concept the same and that was to create seven residential units. After re-design the QS did a revised bill of quantities, we removed certain elements to be client supply items and the contractor agreed to stick to tendered rates, we managed to value engineer the project to a contract figure of £675,000. There was profit in the project, but our contingency was gone, except for additional quantities we had still built into the BOQ.

We agreed to an eight-phase completion with a slightly longer overall project program, this was submitted with the tender. This is important; always ensure you have a contract program in place at the outset (phases were two weeks apart, with one for each residential unit and the outside space). All of this went in the contract.

The Contractor – A limited company with 40 years of trading and a good reputation

The Contractor turned out to be a nightmare. The weather was very unkind, starting in January it was the wettest winter for 10 years, however due to deliberate and continuous program and project management and strict commercial control we made progress, albeit slowly. I was on site three days a week, did weekly meetings with the contractor and formal monthly meetings including the bank representative and QS. Everything was minuted and we recorded weekly what was achieved, what had not started and what was late. These documents were submitted formally and signed for.

It turned out that the management structure in the contractors business relied on one person, who had a nervous breakdown soon after the work started on site and the business then started to fall apart quickly. We had a series of supervisors on site, none of whom managed to fully grasp the task at hand and the project program slipped week after week.

It turns out that the construction company's other sites were also suffering. Sub-contractors were not getting paid and materials suppliers stopped deliveries until payments were received. Although there were warning signs throughout, this came to light when we were two thirds the way through the project and three quarters of the way through the contract, six weeks from phase one hand over - the first of the eight phases.

Project management

Every instruction given on site was given in writing and entered into a log, this may seem laborious, but when things start to go wrong the records need to be there and it is equally important that you comply with the contract as well as the contractor.

The contractor put in place a hired project manager, who was a good man and wanted to do a good job, he had little or no support from the company, who were firefighting on all fronts. We agreed to work together along with the QS to manage the company to get the project completed. We were keeping a 5% retention against all payments and we started, with the company's approval to pay subcontractors directly and pay suppliers for materials to ensure delivery. We knew the project would be late but felt we could get it to limp over the line. A better result than having to get a new contractor part way through a complex project that was not without other issues.

Another nightmare

Just at this stage we had a serious blow with the top section of the three-storey building being condemned, (bear in mind we had done a full strip out and inspection and I had missed this issue, with all of my years of experience. The timber frame was solid from the inside but rotted from the outside with most timbers only 25mm on the inside being in good condition). The walls to the top third of the main building above the cobb walls needed to be replaced completely whilst jacking up the roof timbers. The structural engineer was too busy to deal with the matter for about six weeks; just what the contractor needed to justify an extension of time! So, I agreed with the structural engineer a method of work, did all the drawings, took them to him for approval and at the same time got approval from the building control officer. All sorted within a week, no special materials, blocks timber and insulation. We put in a special order to get materials to site quickly.

As we had averted any delays to the project, by providing a simple quick approved solution and using materials that we had rates for, we avoided any delays beyond the one week and actually saved money on the works originally costed.

In fact there were four construction nightmares, this being only one!

And there was more to come

So you would think that was it right? Well no. We continued to administer the contractor to the letter issuing instructions in writing and by this stage I was producing a weekly program showing delays against the baseline contract program and recording man hours, all signed for by the contractor as verified information, effectively issued by them to me.

I took away issues that were proving difficult to resolve, such as arranging utilities, always only after a letter requesting assistance and accepting that they remained responsible.

Each phase completion date that was missed had a late completion certificate issued and signed for by the contractor. Crucially I did two extension of time (EOT) documents, submitted as required by the contract (I made one mistake, but luckily got away with it as submission of a second EOT, nullifies any previous delay certificates under the contract): I was however able to prove, due to phased completion that the new EOT did not materially change the outcome and it stood.

At each meeting I confirmed that the client retained their right to charge liquidated damages and clearly outlined the extent of the effect of late completion at least monthly. We used the influence of the fellow directors in the SPV to pile on pressure when needed as well.

Almost four months after supposed completion we were very close to completion having nursed the contractor along. I had gone on holiday, believing that the work would be nearly completed on my return. On return I found the contractor had gone into administration closely followed by enforced liquidation.

So no labour available, sub-contractors, threatening to rip out their work due to non-payment, commitments to purchasers of units sold off plan; this left me in an unenviable situation, where I rolled up my sleeves, did some snagging myself and found local tradespeople to finish off the works, Actually it was not as bad as it first looked.

We financially managed the completion and beyond

Because we had withheld a retention of 5% and on the last payment had deducted liquidated damages, we had cash in hand to pay off certain sub-contractors who had cooperated and do deals with specialist contractors to get guarantees and warranties in place. I managed to get building control sign off and properties were ready on dates agreed with purchasers.

What transpired was that I had to personally manage the defects liability period (DLP) and get works sorted out to keep the owners happy.

All the above, as well as dealing with a liquidator who kept moving the goalposts. We put in a claim that the contractor owed us money for works not completed and DLP works. Eventually we managed to agree to cancel our claim against a guarantee that they (the liquidator) would not claim from us. This however took a long time and there were legal and accountancy costs to pay.

We still made a profit

But guess what? We delivered the project for less than the tender figure and all the investors made the returns that were shown in the initial pre investment details. The only negative was my sanity and the ROI being over four years instead of two years!

Lessons learnt:

- Do your homework, prepare well, ensure you have strong and appropriate documentation and project manage the job closely to ensure that you keep control and do not let the project control you (as far as possible).
- Don't take on too large a project unless you have the experience and drive to see it through, no matter what.
- Ensure you have the right project team around you to handle what is likely to happen and for those unforeseen issues that make property so interesting.

Managing Refurbs and Contractors

By Roy Inman

I was sat there looking back over a refurbishment and wondering how did the cost go from £16,000 to over £25,000 without me even realising and not even having any paperwork to show for it?

I bought the property knowing that it needed a refurb and I'd already done a few refurbs so wasn't concerned about it. A few things came up that I hadn't been aware of nor factored in, but that wasn't the main thing that changed the price. It wasn't that I expected it to be £16,000 as I had factored in a contingency for extra costs. £16,000 was just the original quote I had been given but also included the work that I had not realised needed doing.

It needed everything. It needed full electrics. It needed a full central heating system. It also needed full windows, and doors throughout, a new bathroom suite and kitchen. That wasn't all, there was a requirement to drop the front elevation internal leaf wall and rebuild along with new joists and floorboards. If you don't know what an internal leaf wall is, when you think about an exterior house wall that has a cavity in, it is built with two walls and a gap in the middle.

Now you may be thinking, £16,000 for all that work - you're out of your mind. It was going to go way over that anyway. This was in 2004 so refurbs were a lot cheaper back then. This lesson isn't about the price, it's about the contractor, how he played me and how I allowed myself to get sucked in and hopefully you won't make the same mistake.

It was a big refurb, it was the biggest one that I'd done so far and as I stood in the footings of the front reception room of this 2-bed terrace, I was looking up and I could see the ceiling of the bedroom above me. There was no floor or ceiling. I had several quotes that I went through, and for some of the potential contractors it seemed like it was out of their depth and they weren't really sure of what they were doing. I spoke to one contractor who seemed to know what he was doing, had the right contacts and could handle the work, his quote wasn't the cheapest but still reasonable and after looking at some of his previous work I decided to go with him.

He started the project, stripping out and cracking on quite well which was great and it all seemed to be going well. He was overseeing project management and making sure that everything was done, having the brick layer there, and organising everything that was required.

After a few weeks things slowly started to change, he started to change what we had agreed up front with regards to payment being at a halfway point and the end of the project to needing to be paid weekly so that he could then pay the contractors and buy materials. At the time I didn't really have a problem with the materials side of it but he was now so far into the project that I just wanted to keep it going and get it done. It all seemed to be progressing well, so I decided to go with it and agreed.

Most of the refurbs that I'd done previously probably took four to six weeks, this one was going to take between eight and 10, maybe a little bit longer. I'd never worked with this guy, but everything seemed to be moving along nicely. It was fairly early on in my property investing career, I was only 24, and I had been investing for about three years whilst working fulltime as a chef and had around nine buy to let properties.

It then came to the first weekly payment and things changed again, I turned up at the house to pay him with the cheque all written out and he said he needed it in cash, now this hadn't been discussed but he needed cash to pay his contractors as Friday was payday, so off to the bank I went to get cash.

This went on for a number of weeks, some weeks, things would progress really, really, well and everything would be great, and I didn't have too much of an issue handing the money over, then it didn't seem like things had progressed very far at all, but he still wanted the same amount of money.

Before I knew it, the project had dragged on, delay after delay and we had got to a point where not much money was owed but a lot was still left to be done on the project. I had allowed myself to be sucked into excuses and delays and he was now asking for more money to finish the project and I was now stuck between a rock and a hard place with not really anywhere to go. Do I kick him off the project and try to find someone else to finish it? I know that builders hate taking over from another builders unfinished work/project. Do I push forward and hopefully get it finished? At this stage I wanted it finished, I wanted to get it up and running and to get the rental income coming in instead of money just pouring out.

In the end, I agreed to continue the project with him with a small amount payable in a week's time and the rest of the final figure we had agreed paid once the job was finished and complete and I'm happy to say that it did get finished even if it was 50% (£9,000) over budget. Now in the last 16 years of owning it, I've had over £80,000 of rental income and have approximately £50,000 of equity.

Would I go through that again and was it worth it? Yes! Would I do it differently? Hell yes! What we now do is make sure that everything is in writing, we always have a detailed list of scheduled works that is included in the quote. If there are going to be any additional costs during the project, we get a breakdown in writing before confirming that we are happy to go ahead with them and we have a set completion date. All our refurbs now come either within the original costing or a little over unless something major and unforeseen comes up that no one could have really known about until you get into the job and uncover it. We haven't had a major problem with contractors that we couldn't resolve in over 10 years now (touch wood!). Another top tip is to always make sure that you keep a large chunk of money back for the end payment so that they have a good reason to come back and finish the job. If you hold too little back and they feel that it's not worth the hassle and walk away from the last payment you are left high and dry.

Chapter 8

Random Stories: 2

Unbelievable Utilities

By Jackie Tomes

Splitting utilities is a painful and expensive endeavour that requires the local supplier to come and upgrade the supply, a certified tradesman to prepare the internal supply ready for the new connection (i.e. a qualified electrician, plumber, etc.), and in the case of electricity and gas you also need a utility company to come and connect the external supply to your internal wires and install a meter for you. On the project that I had my biggest utility nightmare with, there were issues with both the water and electricity supplies, but it was the electricity that caused the biggest problems.

The first step was bringing around Utility Company A to survey the site and to confirm what they would require to be in place for them to be able to run the upgraded supply to the building. This part went well! I then had Utility Company B come around to confirm exactly what needed to be in place for them to install the meters. This also went well as I had the opportunity to really dig down to what they wanted to ensure that everything was ready for them. Because now we come to the real crux of the matter. The primary issue with upgrading your electric supply is that once Utility Company A have installed the new supply, you then have no electric to the building until the utility company are able to visit to fit the meters and connect you up. Therefore, if anything goes wrong and they aren't happy to install, then you are left with no electricity on your building site until the issue is resolved and they can revisit.

Well, that doesn't sound too hard (I thought). I used a respectable and certified electrician to certify all internal works (whom I'd used plenty of times before), and I made sure that I'd understood exactly what Utility Company B meant by "all electrics must be at least 90% complete" and followed their instructions to the letter before booking a date for Utility Company A to cut our supply, and then another date for the new meters to be installed by Utility Company B two days later. Well the big day arrived, and I was quietly confident. I'd triple checked everything with everyone and done everything we'd been told, what could go wrong?

How wrong was I?

Utility Company B arrived and within five minutes had walked straight back out saying that they weren't happy to install and that we would need to rebook.

What had I done wrong? Well don't worry they were very clear about it, apparently, we hadn't properly secured the hole where the wires exited the distribution box in order to stop children (or adults with very small hands) from putting their fingers in there. I literally couldn't believe it. This was a ridiculous reason for refusing to install the meters as it was something that could easily have been resolved after the meters had been fitted. Also, I could not understand why if that was the safety rule, then how come the distribution box was made and sold in that way? Not to mention the fact that the whole set up was legally required to be contained in a lockable electricity cupboard that children should be unable to access anyway. But nevertheless, this was an easy fix, and once sorted they said they would definitely be able to install the meters next time.

It was fixed within 45 minutes. But unfortunately, we couldn't book another visit for a further two weeks! During which time we were left without any electricity to the site for the building works to continue. We were about to hire an extremely expensive generator to keep the works going for the next two weeks, but thankfully the shop next door allowed us to run an extension cable out their back window and into our building giving us some electricity for £10 per day. But this set up was a nightmare of wires and cables that made working harder and slower so not something we wanted to be doing long term.

Anyway, the next time they visited they were happy with the distribution box but it took them about two more minutes to discover that we hadn't earthed our gas meters, something that no one had ever mentioned needing to be done prior to the meters being installed! They refused to wait for our electrician to come and do the 10-minute job, walking out again saying that once that was sorted, they would 100%, definitely be able to install the meters. Thankfully this time it was only a week till the next available slot.

Unfortunately things didn't get any better as the next time they weren't happy with some of our light fittings, and the time after that they weren't happy with the fireproof board, we'd used to mount our distribution board on, and on and on it went always promising that it was only that one thing that needed fixing, and never being happy to wait while the problem got resolved.

In total I had six visits by Utility Company B over an eight-week period, during which time work slowed way down costing an extra £600 in electricity costs. A very painful experience!

Accidents Lead to Accidents

By Angelos Sanders

For the record, this experience was my own silly fault. One of my refurbs was coming along nicely with lots of work happening whilst converting this run-down property into much larger flats. I am not afraid of getting stuck in sometimes and helping my team as I enjoy the process. One visit on a nice summer's day ended up with lots of sadness. One of my labourers wanted a hand moving an old cardboard box to the back for disposal. I volunteered and walked backwards down the metal stairs holding the box with him holding the other end. As I was about to step onto the last step, my foot gave way and I twisted my ankle. I did not want to show my pain as I was in front of the team for fear of embarrassment, but I could not hold it in. It really was painful. I hobbled home and then was taken to hospital where I was given crutches and ordered to rest.

As I love to see the progress of my sites, I could not be kept away for too long, especially at that stage of the refurb. I wasn't in a position to drive, so I asked my friend one evening to drive me there and see the progress on site. I hobbled into his car and off we went. I got out of the car and decided to leave my crutches in the car as I would hop around, despite my friend's warning not to. You might be thinking, what a hero, what a Superman! More like, what a plonker! I was pleased with the progress and was hopping back to the car when I tripped over a loose floorboard and things went downhill fast.

I fell headfirst and instinctively threw my arms forward wanting to grab anything I could that would save me from smashing my face in and adding to the list of already damaged body parts. Unfortunately (or fortunately), the closest thing to me was my friend's legs. I grabbed them, and I managed to pull his shorts down!

Tips? Don't be a plonker and visit site when recovering from a twisted ankle and always wear the correct PPE.

A Stinker of a House

By Angelos Sanders

I am sure some of us have experienced a bit of unpleasant odour in a house now and again. Whether it is the smell of damp, animal odours or the result of eating too many beans. None of this compares to the absolute stench at this next property.

In my experience when refurbishing many run down and smelly properties, the people living there do not start off living in such a disgusting way. It usually starts with a slow deterioration of standards and probably involves a non-caring landlord and combined, these two issues compound into a smelly property which is unloved and unkempt. The people living in this property had unfortunately fallen into this cycle and had lived there for around 20 years.

To give you an idea of how bad the stench was, I had a letter complaining about the smell and squalid conditions of the place, and that was just from the rats living there. In all seriousness, the tenant was a hoarder in this 6-bedroom property, and I could not even see some of the walls due to the amount of stuff in the property when I was viewing it.

When you opened the bathroom door, what you saw was half eaten dog food, half rotten, in the bath, so that would explain some of the smell. When the rip out started, the guys had to wear hazmat suits to guarantee their safety. We found some old DVDs featuring scantily clad ladies, mountains of pizza boxes, old and fresh dog poo and decomposed rats that had decomposed on the carpets. Once the mountain of belongings had been taken away, the walls and I could finally see one another for the first time and it was not a pretty sight.

The bedroom walls were black with thick mould. When I say black, I mean there was no colour on the walls except black – it was covered like a bad smelling blanket. In these situations, one questions oneself as to how they got into this predicament and their life choices, but you have to be solutions focussed in this industry; there is always a way forward.

The solution here was to bleach the hell out of it. Off I went to the local supermarket and bought up all their bleach stock (around 20 bottles) and the person at the checkout asked what I was going to do with all the bleach. I replied saying that I have had enough of life (tongue firmly in cheek and no, I do not advocate ending lives with bleach).

Back I went to the mouldy house and sprayed the walls with concentrated bleach and sure enough, after a short while, the wall's true colour was revealed – it was mustard yellow – thank you bleach!

The House That Almost Collapsed

By Angelos Sanders

Where do I begin?

I have experienced many interesting challenges in my time as an investor but this next property was the closest I have been to being broken but me being me, I was not going to let that happen no matter what problems the building threw at me.

Background

The building was built circa 1830s and was a beautiful four storey house that was originally built for the high-ranking officers in the Admiralty. Fast forward to the 1950s, and it was converted into flats. Over the decades that followed, it slowly deteriorated and was sold to me in its then current condition.

There were a number of issues that I identified during the conveyancing phase and were provisioned for in the quote from the builder. There was the usual 20% contingency added for the unknown and what a big unknown it turned out to be! More on that a little later. Let us run through the accounted for issues first.

Accounted for issues

Building was almost condemned by the Council

There were problems before the purchase even began. The Council were unhappy with the lack of sufficient heating, insulation, and a number of safety issues in parts of the property. I had to reassure the Council that these issues would be remedied during the refurb and they were happy with that for a fixed period of time.

Joist issues

Imagine a soup bowl or a ski slope - this is what you experienced when walking on the floor inside the property. The floors were very springy when you walked on them and there was a noticeable bowl-shaped look to them. This told me that either the floor joists were rotten or undersized for the span. Luckily for me, it was both issues.

Once the floorboards were taken up, it was obvious that the joists supporting the floorboards were undersized for the span of the rooms, so they needed to be reinforced. We measured the difference between where the joists were level and straight, across the bowl-shaped dip in the middle of the rooms. The difference was about 10cm or four inches. Where joists were rotten, they were replaced. As an extra precaution, the entire building was treated to prevent future woodworm and rot issues.

Whilst the strengthening of the joists was sufficient, I like to make sure that a belt and brace approach is taken. As the old saying goes "you can only overengineer things once". Beneath the joists, we installed steel beams to further support the joists above. After this was done, the floors were level but also rock solid with no give at all.

Damp everywhere

The bay areas in the front of the building were showing evidence of damp everywhere. Whether it was rain penetrating through the old windows, or through cracks in the external render, it was clearly evident that the internal walls would need to be hacked back to stone and the lintels would need to be replaced. There was also evidence that the wooden beams needed some attention due to their proximity to the damp bays.

Some interesting electrics

The main incoming electric supply to the building was located in the rear of the property. For some reason, this was also where the shower room was as well. I suppose it would be handy if you ever needed to charge your phone whilst having a shower (disclaimer – never charge your phone whilst in the shower). Another issue that was addressed was that we had a little electric shock when switching on or off the lights when it was raining. It turned out that there was no earth cabling to a few of the electric circuits with some of the cabling dating back to World War II. Needless to say, everything was ripped out and the entire building was rewired to the latest electrical standards.

Unaccounted for issue

Going back to the 20% contingency and why it is so important to always factor this into your refurb budget. When exposing the original wooden lintels above the windows on the ground floor bay, it was found that they had the structural integrity of wet cardboard due to many years of damp and decay. No problem, we could easily replace them with concrete equivalents and address the damp issue, or so I thought.

A plan was put in place and the first wooden lintel was carefully removed in the centre of the bay. We then saw that there was a single row of bricks shaped as an arch supporting the stories above. Arches are very strong and have stood the test of time, but the keystone (central most brick and the most important) was cracked and had dropped. It was time to hire some more acrow props very quickly and support this arch as quickly as possible. We exposed the lintels in the three stories above and found similar issues on two more of them. Hope for the best, plan for the worst was my next thought. The best-case scenario was that the bay would support itself (with our help) until a permanent solution could be found. Worst case was the bay collapses and takes half the building with it.

All the key project stakeholders were informed about this issue immediately and then it was time to seek some expert structural advice. The first surveyor said that it was not a matter of 'if' the building will collapse, but 'when' and quickly left the site. The second surveyor took everything in his stride and was not fazed by this problem in the slightest. He walked around the site and inspected everything and listened to our potential solution and after a while, he had a plan. The solution was to build a three-storey high steel structure to pin into the brick bay uprights and support the arches – think of it like a splint for a building. The new steel structure would then be tied back to the main building (remember the new steel beams installed to strengthen the floor joists) using steel beams which would be welded and bolted together. Between the bay uprights, new concrete lintels were also installed.

The steels were ordered and carefully installed. The cracks outside were repaired and the windows were replaced, so the building was watertight again. The existing plaster and render was removed so the internal walls could dry. It took a lot of planning but it all fitted together in the end. Building Control signed everything off and I am pleased to say that there has not been any sign of damp or movement since. It delayed the project by several weeks and cost about 10% of the budget, but I know the building should have no issues for a very long time.

Lessons learnt:

- Be very adaptable to any situation and always work with a strong team to overcome difficult challenges.
- Inform key people as soon as possible and try to present a solution to them as well as the initial problem.
- Always have a decent contingency allocated in your budget.

When Retaining Walls Fail

Mike Foulkes

As a Structural Engineer practicing in Cornwall, retaining walls are the bane of my life or more specifically historic stone built retaining walls are.

From time immemorial early Stone Age farmers would have used stones that were abundant on the ground in this part of the world, to build banks to control their livestock. The remains of Stone Age hut circles can still be seen on Bodmin Moor where the topsoil has been removed to produce a round excavation, which were lined internally with field stones to both retain the external ground and support a roof structure of branches tied at their apex similar to a tepee. Although often laid dry, any mortar used between the stones would have been confined to a moist soil dug locally to the site.

With the discovery of iron in around 3500BC, more sophisticated tools became available which allowed the softer stone found on the south coast of Cornwall to be shaped (to some extent). The harder igneous rocks such as granite found on areas of the north coast and the moors were more resistant to working. The shaping of the stones allowed the thickness of the clay mortar beds to be reduced.

Although this allowed the construction of stronger walls there was little need to build walls to retain ground higher than approximately 2.5 metres which is the typical height of a single story of a domestic or small commercial property.

However the coming of the railways in the 1880s saw a huge upheaval in the life of Cornish coastal towns. Prior to the railways the function of the towns would have been confined to providing the export of mineral ores being mined in the hinterland and fishing on a relatively small scale. After the towns were linked by the railway network, the affluent city middle classes could access these otherwise remote areas within a few hours. This created a demand for holiday/retirement homes on an unprecedented scale. The major obstacle facing the Victorian developers was that the Cornish coastal towns were all sited within very steeply sloping valleys created on the estuaries of the rivers which served the moors.

But with the railways came advances in methods of quarrying and construction available to the Victorian builders. Steam power allowed the stone to be cut but this was an expensive process and therefore reserved for the construction of the walls of more prestigious structures. The strength of mortar was also found to improve with the inclusion of lime into the clay mix.

Faced with the pressures (and the potential profits) of this building boom but emboldened by the improvement in construction techniques, the Victorian builders went to work building roads and houses up the sides of the river valleys. The houses were often built as long terraces. They would typically excavate into the hillside to the rear of the terrace and form a level site by filling the excavated material against a retaining wall constructed to the front of the site. A technique known as 'cut and fill'. The property would be constructed on the firm rock to the rear of the site with the front wall constructed on the edge of the rock platform. The ground between the front façade of the building and the retaining wall (i.e. the front garden) would be loose fill material. The line of the underlying rock would invariably form a diagonal line extending upward from the base of the retaining wall to approximately 600mm or so below the front wall which provided the founding strata for the stonework to the front wall.

The same technique was used for the construction of the access roads to these properties which are often narrow steeply sloping lanes only usable with caution by modern cars.

The retaining walls to the front of the properties were often constructed to five metres or so in height and the cut rock face to the rear would extend to even a greater height. In some cases the rock to the rear of the sites was deemed at the time to be sufficiently robust so as not to require a stone retaining wall and therefore the cutting left a vertical exposed rock face. In other cases, where the rock was more fractured or with undulated bedding planes, a face of stonework was either constructed vertically or at a steep angle against the rock. Often the built stonework was confined just to ledges in an effort to strengthen a local area of weakness within the rock leaving an irregular patchwork of exposed rock and stonework.

The height of the cut rock faces to the rear of the terraces is often breath taking. For example the height of the cutting to rock face adjacent to some properties is so great that it towers over the buildings below.

In many cases walls have been constructed in more recent times on top of the cut rock faces to further level out the gardens of the properties above which exacerbates the scale of the original works. Often these later walls were built by property owners with a substandard, single skin of blockwork with little regard as to what lay many metres below.

The health of these stone retaining walls can be determined by viewing their alignment and the quantity of ground water flowing through the wall. The outward bowing of an area of stonework is an indication that it has delaminated away from its original position. Water flow through the wall or even excessive damp will wash out the clay lime mortar and lubricate the interface between individual stones. Some owners have tried to seal the walls with modern cement-based mortars. This is a double-edged sword. Whilst it may help to lock individual stones in place it inhibits the drainage of water. In these cases the wall is not only proving a retaining structure but is acting as a dam!

The longevity of walls displaying these initial stages of duress can be lengthened by the use of rock anchors and wall plates. This process requires 30mm or so diameter holes to be drilled though the stonework and into the rock face behind and the installation of a steel rod which is resin grouted into the rock and secured to the face of the stonework with steel wall plates. The rock anchors are installed in rows at approximately 1500mm or so centres in both the horizontal and vertical directions.

These walls have reached the end of the useful lives and are now, after 150 years, collapsing. After a period of heavy rain (which is becoming more frequent) my telephone will ring nonstop with the same message of woe.

Once a retaining wall has collapsed it is a question of tidying up the damage caused by the impact of many tons of stone masonry on the building or road below and rebuilding. Rebuilding is usually undertaken using reinforced concrete with rock anchors. The difficulty of the reconstruction process is exacerbated by the limited access to the site for heavy construction plant and concrete lorries.

Where defence of the ground at the base of the wall is less important, reconstruction using a system of rock stitching and steel netting is being used more often.

Many purchasers of the quaint Cornish cottages from 'up country' have learnt about the perils of these retaining walls. In the worst cases, the cost of the reconstruction of the retaining wall defending the site can exceed the original cost of the purchase of the property. Buyer beware!

Summary

Going into a refurbishment project with your eyes open to all possibilities and drawing upon the experiences of seasoned professionals is a must, as the stories in this section have shown.

Below is an 11-Point Pre-Start Building Checklist by Building Control to assist you before you start work. Take a few moments to run through this list as it could make your build a lot easier, saving you time, money and frustrating delays.

1. CIL: Once planning permission is granted you should have been sent a liability notice setting out any Community Infrastructure Levy and when it is due for payment. Before work starts you must submit a 'Commencement Notice' to the Planning Department if your project is liable for CIL. For self builds, have you completed your CIL exemption forms?

2. Planning Conditions: Find out if there are any Planning Conditions. Have they been cleared? Do any need to be cleared before commencement and are any your responsibility? E.g. building sample panels, providing percolation tests, supplying manufacturer's details for materials etc.

3. Decide who you are using for Building Control: Make sure that you have made an application before work starts – it's never too early to talk to your Local Authority Building Control team.

4. Party Wall Act awards: Is there an award in place? Are you aware of any special conditions? This can take a while to sort out and needs to be in place before you start work.

5. Have you got the right drawings? Are the building regulations drawing and planning drawing the same? Check the dimensions, especially boundary distances and heights. Have you got the latest?

6. Is it a Listed Building? Make sure Listed Building Consent has been granted before you start even if planning permission isn't required – the person carrying out the work is the responsible person.

7. Do you need to submit a demolition notice to Building Control?

8. Have you notified the HSE if your project will take more than 30 days?

9. Are there any special Planning Building Regulations issues? E.g. Is it in a water scarcity area? If so, you might need to use special fittings to reduce water usage to 105 litres per person per day – talk to Building Control.

10. Have special access conditions been applied? Is the dwelling designed to meet AD M41, 2 or 3? Ask Building Control if you aren't sure – there are big cost implications if you find out too late.

11. Have you arranged a warranty? You probably need one for a new dwelling. Have you had a quote from LABC Warranty? This is a very viable alternative warranty provider.

PART 3

PEOPLE NIGHTMARES

Introduction

Property is all about people.

Yes, the properties might be built of bricks and mortar, but it is everything that happens within it that really makes any kind of difference. Working with and for people is a skillset quite different to any other. What works one day with one person, doesn't work the next. What works for one person can be quite the opposite with someone else even if they do the same job in the same way. No wonder it can be a head scratcher and sometimes a nightmare.

If the bricks in a property are the structure, then the people involved in any aspect of the property are the cement that holds it all together. We all need a roof over our heads, somewhere where we feel safe and secure. One of the primary purposes of property is to provide homes for people or space for them to work and this section explores when this does not go well.

When dealing with people and property, you can sometimes experience a fascinating array of different situations, some of which you can almost predict and some of which might completely blindside you. The tip is to be always prepared as many conflicts can occur, often from sources that have nothing to do with you. Have you ever been on the receiving end of an unexpected angry phone call that you have tried to calm whilst trying to understand the source of frustration? How easy is it to move to defend yourself when you feel attacked? Yet on reflection, you realise that the person who was angry was angry because of something else that had gone wrong for them before you called; you just became someone they could vent at.

This section covers the weird and wonderful world that can emerge when people do not necessarily get on well with their properties or the agents involved with looking after those properties. It is not always easy owning or renting property as the property sometimes fights back and creates lots of problems and, if left unchecked, it can descend into a world of misery. It is that misery that this section covers in detail but most importantly, the solutions, which will help people avoid similar mistakes.

Whether it is rogue tenants or rogue landlords, buyers or sellers, there are lessons here to help anyone involved in property.

The stories in the People Nightmares section cover:

- Tenants
- Landlords and letting agents
- The great condensation vs. damp debate
- Assassins!

Chapter 9

Tenants

The Sad Story of the Squatter

By Angelos Sanders

This is a story of a father's love for his daughter.

I bought an abandoned property that had a basement. The property had been vacant for around two years but during that time, there were squatters living there and one of the squatters decided to live in the basement. The property was in a terrible state with needles and excrement everywhere, so the newly arrived squatter must not have been too impressed with the condition. He proceeded to tidy up the basement.

When the previous official tenant had left the basement, they had flooded the place so that when you walked in, you were hit with an overwhelming smell of damp with orange mushrooms growing on the walls. The walls were painted dark red and there was no carpet or underlay. To the credit of the squatter, he had tidied the place up quite well and made the place look presentable. He collected the rubbish and put it into black sacks and apart from the stench and the lack of carpet, it was almost liveable.

He furnished the bedroom with an old mattress on the floor, and in front of the mattress was a child sized plastic toy table. On the table were various dolls standing up, neatly arranged. On the edge of the table were four pink baby dummies lined up in a row; it seemed that he was looking to create a sense of order and homeliness in this tough situation.

When the agent took me around to view the property, they told me an ex-prisoner had been released and had nowhere to live, and so he found this property and started squatting within it. He had his daughter visit occasionally. To think that the young child would be living in those conditions really does make you think, but then again, when you have nothing and you feel desperate and you need to see your child, what else can you do? It was quite sobering walking around there with the team and we all had a greater appreciation for what we had compared to other people less fortunate than ourselves.

There is a happy ending to this tale though. The agent informed told me that the Police were called as he was squatting and because he wasn't necessarily in the best frame of mind and with no support anywhere, they took him and gave him a nice meal, then passed him on to the local Council to try and assist him in creating a new future for himself.

Ambush at Night

By Angelos Sanders

Sometimes doing the right thing and helping people can actually get you into some pretty precarious situations. There are certain property purchases where you inherit some tenants who, during the course of their long stay, have allowed the condition of the property to become really run down. This story is about one such property.

This particular seller was living abroad and was very reliant on the letting agent doing the right thing by informing the tenants that the property was for sale and that there was a possibility that they may have to be moved on. Two of the tenants realised that the property was being sold and no longer wanted to live in such a squalid condition but one of the tenants decided that they were going to do some works to improve their property. During a prearranged viewing there seemed to have been a bit of a mix up with the communication with the tenants. Apparently, they had not been told that the property was on the market and they thought that we were simply looking to let another flat. It was left to me to explain that I was viewing it with a view to buying it and that there would need to be a series of works to bring the property up to standard. The tenant burst into tears as they had no idea that this was going to happen and were spending a lot of money on a refurb. I felt sorry for the tenant as it was not in any way, shape or form their fault. The owner of the property really should have informed all of their tenants, but the situation was that I had broken the news to them rather than the owner, and therefore it fell to me to try and reassure the tenant that things would work out fine for everyone.

The property itself was in an atrocious condition. There was wallpaper hanging off the walls, the lights were not working as someone had attempted some DIY alterations, which blew out the fuses. I said to the tenants that the property was being sold to myself and we were going through the conveyancing process, which could take a couple of months and that would give us enough time to help move them onto more respectable accommodation.

Usually when I help tenants I inherit and intend to help move along, I try to make their lives as easy as possible. I help them find alternative accommodation and pay for their move and most importantly, keep them up to date with the various things that are happening, including giving realistic time frames as to when and how things will move forward. This process, which at the start can be a little tense, usually leads to the tenants understanding that I need to refurbish the property and therefore it could only be to their advantage to take me up on my offer of assistance and find somewhere much better for them. On this particular occasion it was not so smooth. With the owner's permission I was able to negotiate with the tenants in this particularly bad property and we would be on hand to help them as much as possible.

It took approximately three months for the conveyancing to take place as the seller needed to get retrospective planning approval and it also gave the tenant and I plenty of time to help find alternative accommodation. Remember, I was acting as the seller's agent as he was abroad. With the estate agent's permission, I was able to lead the negotiation with the tenant to ensure that it was a win-win scenario for all parties concerned. Ultimately, I wanted a vacant house so I could begin work straight away and I also wanted the tenants to be happy. A completion date was agreed with the seller and I informed the tenants that in a short space of time that I would be getting the keys and becoming the new owner and that they needed to make a start on the moving process.

Unfortunately during the conveyancing process and despite what I was being told by the tenants, other ideas had popped into their head and other than what had been agreed in their favour. They wanted a considerable amount of money to move on at the last minute. Notice had been served properly and the seller was within his rights to begin eviction proceedings should they have felt it necessary, but we didn't want to go down that road because he would only cause the tenants stress and everyone would lose time and money and that would not benefit anyone. However the owner did not want to be held hostage by the tenants either.

I relayed the tenant's financial request to the seller who was very hostile to the request as he had not been paid rent in many months and was not very amenable to the idea of negotiating at all. So there I was playing piggy in the middle trying to negotiate between the seller (who was not happy because he felt aggrieved by the request especially as the tenants had not paid their rent for many months) and the tenants (who were living in very poor conditions feeling also upset that they were not getting a good deal out of this). I eventually managed to persuade the seller to open their wallet and meet the tenant halfway with their financial demands to help bring this matter to a close.

The seller reluctantly agreed and I relayed this back to the tenant who was holding out until the day of completion and agreed to what was being offered to them. The agreement was as follows. On the day of completion, I would meet the tenant at 5:00 PM, give the tenant the money and in exchange, they would give me their keys and move on. Returning of keys is academic as the locks are always changed on the day of completion.

I arrived at the house at 5:00 PM and I was greeted by seven agitated people outside the house including the tenant. This lovely gent approached me, wanting to have a fight because of the way he believed his family member had been mistreated. He was obviously defending his family members' honour and I completely understood his posturing but I had to try and diffuse the situation. I looked him straight in the eye and said the following.

"Whilst I understand you're clearly angry at this situation, and I would feel exactly the same, I'm not the owner/seller, and I'm the one here now with you with the money to try and help give your family member a new start in life and move out of this rat-infested property."

The tenant then turned to her family members and said this person has tried to help me and it's not his fault and things then calmed down, with the angry guy even shaking my hand afterwards for helping. They gave me the keys and they were given the money and that was the end of that situation. The property was now officially mine and was ready for works to begin.

The lesson is that if you want something badly enough, then you have to persevere through many different challenges and sometimes even have to act as the United Nations.

Hugging Your Way Out Of Trouble

By Francis Dolley

She paced across the stage with an air of authority and what I later realised was an inbuilt determination to stay calm and resilient no matter what life threw at her. I was feeling completely out of place at my very first property seminar, a massive auditorium in London. The experienced investor was winding up her talk and regaling the enthusiastic audience with a few 'tales from the trenches' and the reality of what it was really like to be a landlord. Several times during her 45-minute talk she said, "Property investing isn't really about property at all, it's all about people". At that time I had no idea what she was talking about, but over the coming years I came to come to understand exactly what she meant.

My first rental property used to be my family home. It was a three-bed-room cottage with a large, attached garage to one side, which I converted into a two-bedroom flat. The very first tenancy lasted all of three weeks and was a complete baptism of fire. This was around a decade ago and over the years, I bought many more two and three bed houses in the same little town, before I changed direction and set up several much larger multi-let properties in a nearby bigger town. When progress became too slow for my liking (I wanted more cash flow and I wanted it now!) I decided to give Rent 2 Rent my complete focus until I reached my new much larger cash flow goal. Our Rent 2 Rent business, of which I'm co-Director, now manages 28 large and lovely multi-let properties and is totally systemised. More recently I launched my first holiday let; one of three in a complex which I hope to have finished by the end of the year. After that, who knows?

As you can imagine, over this time I have come into contact and dealt with many property people; fellow investors, agents, surveyors, solicitors, colleagues, mentors, tradesmen, employees and most of all, tenants. To say that all tenants are difficult would not be correct to say as we have had many amazing and totally lovely people stay in our properties. But as Murphy's Law dictates; what can go wrong, will go wrong, and usually at the worst possible moment. At one time the universe was sending me so many difficult people masquerading as tenants, that I thought someone must be sticking pins into my voodoo doll effigy!

Before I relate the tale of the first two tenants to you, I must first say that some of my tenancies have been completely uneventful, like my first two-bed purchase which I eventually sold after seven years. The house was pretty much maintenance free and had one perfect tenant the whole time I owned it. She kept the place looking great and never once complained about anything. I bought it for £72k and sold it five years later for £120k, so a profit of £48k. A new theatre and car park had been built on waste ground right behind this house and the property had been allocated a parking space, which increased the value of the house by approximately £10k. It was a lovely little house and I was a little bit sad to see it go, but I had other plans for the money, including going travelling in South America for a month.

The property in question was my second purchase; an ordinary mid-terrace two bed house needing a light refurb. My first customers rented it for six months and neglected to tell me that the boiler's water pressure had dropped (due to a small leak under the kitchen sink), causing the boiler to stop working. This meant that for the winter they spent at the property, they had neither heating nor hot water. I only discovered this when they were checking out at the start of February and was totally aghast. I went to my vehicle and got a spanner (I always had my maintenance bag handy) and fixed the problem within 30 seconds. As we walked around checking the inventory, the house started warming up and the departing tenants started changing their mind about leaving. The second occupants stayed for eighteen months. Their tenancy was completely uneventful; they looked after the property and always paid on time, but sadly the parents split up and moved on. The third tenancy was a completely different story.

It's always a tough call trying to judge a person's character and their ongoing ability to fulfil a long-term financial obligation to you, from a brief meeting in an empty property, but that's often what we as landlords must do. I always referenced potential tenants but also relied a lot on 'gut-feeling' to help me make my decision. Scientists are telling us that the gut is now thought to be our third 'brain' (the heart being the second one), and though my gut feeling was often correct, it's not infallible.

I had three couples apply for the house; including a flamboyant couple about to open a tattoo shop. They were great; lots of 'ink' and nose-rings but sadly no job security, no guarantors, and no idea if their business would be a success. Then there was the long-distance lorry driver and his 'wife', only they really didn't seem like a couple to me and I thought she might have been a decoy to help him to secure the tenancy, as his earnings were too sporadic on their own. I concluded she was probably a good friend or maybe his sister. I should have asked them to have a snog to prove they were a couple. There was also a guy from a local kebab house who wanted to pay six months upfront, which always sets off alarm bells with me, and it didn't take long to discover that this gentleman was currently being evicted from a house just up the road for, wait for it, unpaid rent. I discovered this by speaking to the neighbours, which are always a good source of information.

So that left just one couple; no pets, no kids, they both had steady jobs, could provide references and this would be their first house together. They seemed perfect. When I met them for the first time, and indeed any consequent time thereafter, the guy shook my hand (this was pre-Covid) as one normally would. The lady however, skilfully side-stepped my outstretched hand and went straight in for a hug, which quickly evolved into more of a giggly cuddle, and she wouldn't let go! It was kind of sweet and just a tiny bit creepy at the same time, as it went on w-a-y too long. I assumed her social skills were a bit mixed up or she was trying to impress me with her friendliness. A week later they moved in and like many people, as soon as they started living together, they discovered that the other one had a load of habits they didn't much like (and after being in close proximity to him several times, I surmised it may have been partly due to his hit-and-miss personal hygiene standards). They soon fell out and he started sleeping in the other room around the same time she called me to announce she was pregnant. This was also around the time the 'fun and games' started in earnest. Over the next seven months I was summoned to the house on a weekly basis to sort the 'severe maintenance issues'. This consisted initially of a grubby pull cord in the bathroom which she deemed was a health risk (!) and the lounge door handle that wasn't a match for the other handles, that sort of thing. I would call my local handyman and ask him to swing by and sort these 'issues' on his way home. After his first visit he called me and asked, "Does she hug you?" I assured him this was perfectly normal. Over time she became more and more agitated as I didn't attend to these 'maintenance issues' in person, and so after the baby was born, she decided to up the stakes to force my attendance.

The first call was to tell me the kitchen floor tiles (professionally laid just four years previously) had 'exploded up'. I arrived at the property (had the usual full-on hug) to find that someone had smashed around thirty of the kitchen floor tiles! The lady told me they all had come loose and then broke when she stood on them. I was accompanied by the handyman and we both agreed this could never have happened in a million years, and in fact you could clearly see hammer marks on the broken tiles. The very next day we replaced all the broken tiles with the best match we could find, which was in fact an altogether different colour, as that range of tiles had been discontinued.

The next call was to tell me a chunk of the bedroom ceiling had fallen down. I was away so again, the handyman inspected it and sent me photos of the damage. We both agreed once again it was obviously done with a hammer. He repaired it straight away but early the next morning she called me again to say his repairs had fallen out. This was an absolute impossibility.

I arrived at the property (endured a quick and somewhat awkward hug) to meet her and her concerned parents who were there as back-up. I calmly explained that the possibility of the floor exploding up and the ceiling falling down (twice) a few days later, was off the Richter scale and an absolute impossibility. Her mum asked if I was calling her daughter a liar and her dad sheepishly looked at the floor. Once again, the handyman got his tools out and mended the hole in the bedroom ceiling.

Over the next few months chunks of plasterboard ceiling mysteriously 'fell down' in another six (!) locations all over the house, and every time I made sure the repairs were always completed within twenty-four hours. It was getting to be like a game of cat and mouse. All the time the hugs continued. One day I was speaking with a fellow investor who told me my tenant was probably trying to make it look like it was a dangerous house and that I was a bad landlord, this way she would get to the top of the 'families-at-risk' register and be much more likely to be offered a Council house. Of course!

One Friday afternoon, when I had heard nothing all week and thought maybe she'd finally given up, she sent me photos which showed over 50% of the kitchen ceiling now residing on the recently repaired two-tone kitchen floor. This was a fairly new plasterboard ceiling which would now require completely replacing. Enough was enough and I called her ex-boyfriend, who had now moved out. He told me part of the reason they broke up was that she was very temperamental.

By now she had also involved the Environmental Health department so I got straight on the phone to the officer and explained what had been going on over these past six months. I also informed the officer of my intention to sell this property, so I would be giving the tenant a Section 21 notice. I've found that no matter how glaringly obvious it is that a tenant is at fault, the Council will nearly always take their side against the 'evil' landlord.

So I had to make sure that I did everything by the book, as I always do. This was only my second eviction (the first one left before the court appearance) and so I hired an eviction expert to make sure there were no mistakes. The Council and the tenant (probably with free legal aid assistance) tried to catch me out several times, questioning my paperwork, but all to no avail as I had crossed all my T's and firmly dotted all my I's. Departure day arrived, the tenant left as requested and miraculously the ceilings stopped falling down. Funny that.

I had bought this property at a 20% discount for £80k and sold it for £109k; a clear profit of £29k. Even with the multiple ceiling repairs over the last six months, this had still been a great little investment. After being hands-free from tenants for so long, I was reminded that a major downside of hands-on property management is the tenants who constantly try to take away your time with trivial issues, and time is the one thing that cannot ever be replaced.

In conclusion: Some tenants are a joy to know and they brighten your day whenever you see them. Then there is the other kind; the kind that causes the sun to dim, the birds to stop singing and whenever you see them, you get a chill in your spine and the smell of sulphur fills the air. Property is a 'people' business for sure!

Cleopatra the Assassin

By Angelos Sanders

It is not every day that you come across some real history associated with a building. The building itself was built in about 1830 and had experienced a very varied history. It was a five-storey building which originally would have been a grand house that would probably have housed an officer in the Royal Navy. Over the years it was converted into a multi-let, which became slum-like in the 1950s and 1960s, and more recently had been converted into flats that were in a very run-down condition.

In I went with the builder and we scoped out a significant schedule of works. As the rip out crew were carefully dismantling things, there was a box in the top left-hand side of an alcove which didn't have any access port, or function; it was purely a box in the corner of the room on the ceiling which made no sense whatsoever. We were intrigued. We carefully opened up this box to see what was inside. To our surprise there were some old Playboy magazines but also there was a remnant from an old newspaper clipping dated to around 1840.

The workers thought it was intriguing and handed this piece of history to me, and then I asked for the newspaper clipping. I carefully held the clipping in my hand and brushed off the dust and soot.

I began reading it and it was a story about a lady called Cleopatra. The story went as follows. Cleopatra's boyfriend had been caught stealing and he ended up in prison. Cleopatra went to visit her boyfriend in prison where he was sharing a cell with another inmate. She made them both a cup of tea and left. The boyfriend and his cellmate began choking and very quickly died.

The alarm was raised and just before Cleopatra managed to exit the prison, the guards stopped her at the entrance as they thought things were a bit suspicious. The prison guards then searched Cleopatra for any evidence of wrongdoing. Now Cleopatra wasn't very smart and when the guards searched her, they found a little sachet on her. The sachet was labelled poison. Now that has to be one of the easiest open and shut cases Police would ever have come across. What lesson can we draw from this story? If you do feel the need to assassinate your boyfriend in prison, do not label the sachet holding the poison beforehand.

The Baby and the Brothel

By Jo Lines

Having worked with tenants and landlords for the best part of 14 years I have certainly come across some nightmare situations. The majority of the issues that escalated were due to communication issues. It has been a steep learning curve and I have certainly learnt how to manage and deal with conflict more effectively.

With regards to communication, I recall an interesting handwritten slip of paper being left on the doorstep of my letting agency. The note read – 'there are some weird smells coming from your property, though we would let you know before we inform the Police'. It was a bit of a mystery to start with as there was no name, address, or detail of which one it was. Two days later the Police arrived – they had had an anonymous tip off about the smell of cannabis coming from one of our properties.

I had heard about tenants having cannabis farms in properties but never did I think it would be in one that I would have to deal with. The Police had entered the property and removed 12 plants that had been in the loft along with the equipment that went with it. When I asked who had been growing it, to my dismay the Police officer gave me a man's name. The tenant we had recently moved in was a single lady who had just had a baby. I went round to visit the property, apprehensive as to who or what I might find. Nobody answered the door. I put a note through the letterbox asking her to call the office. Just as I posted it through, the next-door neighbour came to the door, did you get my note? Now it made sense – I did explain that we managed hundreds of properties and more detail would have helped. As we discussed what had been going on to my horror, she opened my eyes to the nightmare she had been living next to. This was not the first time the Police had been called or even the second but she mentioned over 10 occurrences and she had only been there for about four months.

The lady who was just about to have a baby when she moved in had to claim benefits so we could not get an employer's reference, she came with her mum who was going to act as guarantor. She explained she was a dancer and that she wouldn't be able to go back to work until her baby was about one year old. At this point she seemed fine until her pimp came back on the scene according to the neighbour and had turned the house into a brothel! She had been caught running down the street naked on occasions and having violent fights.

There was a part of me that felt sorry for this young lady and of course her baby and wanted to get her the help she needed. The other part of me was worried about how I was going to sort out the property including the damages and the nuisance she had brought to the neighbours. The battle to rectify this seemed to take forever, the police would not help, social services got involved and the whole thing ended when she tried to take her own life inside the property. I won't go into too much detail but it did look like a crime scene from CSI.

The whole situation was very stressful for everyone involved and emotionally challenging as well as expensive to get the property back to a lettable condition. Working with her family was not easy as they did not have any money and I don't think they were aware of the many issues that happened.

Everything was written down and recorded as evidence and all parties were informed all along the way. In hindsight, how we did our referencing procedure and background checks certainly left room for improvement. As we learnt our lessons the hard way, more due diligence checks were implemented as well as move-in inspections shortly after completion. I project managed the refurbishment and am pleased to say the next tenants that moved in were a delight.

A Pointed Welcome

By Angelos Sanders

Purchasing this particular property was a rollercoaster ride after all the barriers that the seller had placed in front of me, whether it was to show that he was in control of the purchase process by doing everything on his outrageous terms, or whether he was simply scared of being found out at just how shoddy a landlord he truly was. Whatever the reason, it was a great sense of relief to finally hold the keys in my hand.

I texted all the tenants to inform them of my new ownership and to tell them that I wanted to meet up with all seven tenants in the seven flats. I wanted to introduce myself properly and listen to any concerns they had about the property itself. A date and time was agreed with everyone and I turned up and knocked on the door. I was welcomed by the first tenant who seemed nice enough and I listened to his issues. Thanking him for his time, I moved onto the second tenant. No response. Perhaps he was running behind? I would return to him later. I moved onto the next floor and I knocked on the door. "Come in" was the angry reply from inside the flat. The door was unlocked and I entered. The tenant was a large gent who clearly had worked himself up for our meeting with lots of pent-up anger and frustration.

The first thing he said to me was "I want to punch you through the door." I instinctively smiled as I thought he was joking but I quickly realised that he was being deadly serious. One of the first reactions I had was to call his bluff, but I reminded myself that the main objective was to open a constructive dialogue with the man, plus I did not want my new Star Trek Christmas jumper ruined.

The next words out of his mouth were even more shocking. "Actually, instead of punching you, I should have dragged you onto my bed and stabbed you." I replied, "at least I would die on something soft". I then peered into his bedroom and saw the mattress where I might have spent my last few moments on this Earth and realised it was filthy and rotten. At least make the effort to clean the damned thing first before you threaten to stab someone to death!

Once I had diffused the situation and he realised he wasn't necessarily going to intimidate me as he had planned and that I was there to listen and help him, we both sat down and I listened to the source of his frustrations for the next hour. I am not making excuses for his behaviour, but there are always reasons for people's bad behaviour; the key is working out what their motivation is and then you know how to target their pain points with solutions.

It turned out that for the past 15 years he had reported many problems to the previous landlord and no action had been taken to remedy any of the issues. Even his ceiling had collapsed from the damp coming in from a leak of the bathroom from the flat above. People like the previous landlord are the reason why the industry sometimes gets a bad name and then unfortunately everyone is tarred with the same brush. Happily for the tenant, we worked out a plan to quickly resolve his issues with my team and he remained there for many years to come.

Dampness and Condensation

By James Barron

The effects of dampness and condensation are one of the most common issues that a Building Surveyor will come across. The problem with dampness and condensation is that the two are very commonly confused. In this case study we will examine a problem of reported dampness in a flat. This was a ground floor flat within a relatively recently converted building.

I was called in by the managing agent who looked after the building on behalf of a management company. The agent had been getting repeated complaints from an owner about damp within his flat on an external wall. Although this was a ground floor flat, below that there were a series of cellars with light wells running around the outside of the building, allowing a flow of light into the cellar accommodation. This historic building was of solid rubble stone construction dressed externally with limestone and lime jointing, both of which are relatively permeable materials.

The walls were approximately 700 millimetres thick, built with a dressed face of limestone but with a rubble and earth core. The internal face of the wall was battened and dry lined with plasterboard and there was no evidence of any insulation having been fitted behind. The owner of the flat was concerned about damp and mould on the external wall. This was mostly along the line of the ceiling at the top of the wall and around the windows.

A little now about the flat.

There were only four windows, all set within the same external wall. It is not uncommon in converted buildings to find that the flats share a communal core in the centre of the building and then run along one of the buildings external faces. All the windows faced in the same direction, approximately east. There were no trickle ventilators within the window frames and no benefit from any double glazing.

The windows had a stone window reveal, sill and head. The layout of the flat had a kitchen with an open plan living area, a bedroom and a bathroom.

Let's consider now what the dampness might be.

Was it rising damp?

A quick answer to that was no. The walls were very thick and, although the flat was at ground floor level, there was cellar accommodation underneath and a light well running around the outside. This meant that the walls enclosing this flat were well elevated above actual external ground level. Remember that rising dampness can only climb through masonry by about one metre, so this dampness affecting the east wall, particularly at the top of that wall in this flat, could not be rising dampness.

Take checks with a moisture meter.

Moisture meters are readily available but are also very readily misused. It takes experience to understand how to use a moisture meter. Remember that it is a very simple device measuring electrical conductivity between two probes and requires care and experience to interpret.

Moisture meters are calibrated to read 'wood moisture equivalent' (WME) within timber. Using a moisture meter on masonry is useful, but instead of looking simply at the number on the meter, you have to interpret the pattern of readings and understand what that is trying to tell you. I have in the past seen a person in a loft space, convinced that there is dampness tracking through from the neighbours loft into hers, because when she put the probes of a moisture meter onto the brickwork of the chimney breast the readings told her that the wall was damp. In fact, there was no dampness – just the effects of many decades of salts and chemicals penetrating into the bricks through open fires at the property. It was those salts that were sending the meter readings skyward, not dampness.

In the case of this example the readings taken across the east wall in all of the rooms in the flat were consistent. This is useful information. Had this been a problem of rising dampness, I would have expected there to have been a greater concentration of moisture in the lower part of the wall, gradually lessening as the meter climbs up the height of the wall. It's not uncommon to find a tide mark within a wall, even if this can't be seen, by careful use of a moisture meter. That tide mark, i.e. a line where moisture suddenly appears in a wall where it does not exist below or above, sometimes suggests a previous damp proofing treatment that has failed. The dampness is rising above the level of previous treatment.

Now check to see if there is any ventilation.

In this case, ventilation was lacking. The bathroom did have a basic extractor fan fitted into the ceiling with, presumably, a length of ducting running through a false ceiling under the structural floor of the flat above. Because of the layout of the flat the bathroom was in the centre of the building, meaning that the nearest outside wall was about six metres away where there was a vent neatly cut into the stone external wall. A duct of that length, even with booster fans, is likely to be ineffective.

You can test this for yourself. On a calm dry day use a sheet of paper held over the external fan grill. With the fan running, see if the fan is powerful enough to lift the paper away from the wall. In my experience it almost certainly is not. How then is it supposed to quickly empty the bathroom of moisture laden air?

It's very common to find that extractor fans are fitted in kitchens and bathrooms, but that insufficient care and thought has been put into how that moist air is to be vented to the outside. Long lengths of extract hose will simply be ineffective. In this flat the kitchen did have an extractor fan but like many this was a simple re circulation fan filtering out grease and smells. This was not vented to the outside and did nothing to reduce the moisture vapour generated from that room.

Are the windows opened?

Yes, but because this was a ground floor flat the occupants were naturally reluctant to leave the windows ajar when they went to work. I remember discussing this with another surveyor who has considerable expertise in condensation control. His opinion was that the best way to ventilate a property was to open opposite windows every morning for a period of 15 minutes. This would create a total air change through the flat, getting rid of all the moisture vapour in the air which has built up overnight.

Like many flats, there was a fundamental problem with regards to ventilation. As mentioned all of the windows were on one side of the building only. Therefore, it was not possible to create a natural cross flow of air by simply leaving windows open.

Ask yourself where the owners are likely to dry clothes. It's amazing for surveyors to discover how all of the drying clothes seem to disappear when a surveyor comes around! Because there is no communal clothesline or any outside space for this flat, I could only assume that the clothes were dried in a spare room or on radiators.

Have a look to see where the washing machine and tumble dryer are located. In this case there was an internal cupboard with a combined washer dryer. This was within the depth of the flat with no connection to an outside wall. The vent hose from the dryer was simply turned upwards and vented into the cupboard. A huge amount of moisture vapour would be generated from this machine.

Moisture vapour is always generated within properties from cooking, bathing and even breathing. A typical household can easily generate 5kg of moisture laden vapour each day, without adding the effects of cooking and bathing. All of that is held within the air around you.

With extractor fans, always look for the exit position. I have found many examples where extractor fans are not vented to the outside, but instead, the extract hoses have simply been left loose in loft spaces or above kitchen units. Unless they are properly vented to the outside, the moisture vapour they are trying to expel will simply stay within the internal environment.

How does condensation work?

The science is relatively simple. Moisture vapour is held in the air and the amount of moisture vapour will vary, depending on all sorts of environmental conditions. However, it is inevitable that the level of moisture vapour will build up in properties unless it is ventilated to outside.

Moisture vapour in the air condenses when it reaches its dew point. This is the point of temperature where the vapour condenses into droplets of water.

That dew point is first reached on colder parts of the building structure. Think about how the building is put together. In this case, the building had a concrete floor separating the ground floor flat from the first floor flat. That floor was built into the outside stone walls and the massing of concrete and stonework at that connection would cause a line of coldness which, in surveying terms, we call a cold bridge. This would help explain why there was a tendency for the condensation and mould growth to form at the ceiling tops of the walls.

Also, think about the windows. These have stone surrounds where the walls are thinner and single glazing, which naturally makes for a cold bridge in this area.

Consider the orientation of the building. In this case, all of the windows and the wall suffering from 'dampness' were east facing. An east wall will not see any strong sunshine and will tend to stay colder and more sheltered than, say, the south or west facing walls. This makes the east side of a building naturally more vulnerable to the formation of condensation.

The outcome

Having taken site information, collected the evidence and considered the issues, it quite quickly became clear that the problem of dampness was in fact a problem of condensation.

The owners were advised to fit the dryer with an external vent hose or use a condensing machine instead. That is one way to minimise the moisture vapour being created inside the flat. They were advised to have high-capacity extractor fans fitted in the kitchen and bathroom and vented to outside where possible.

Other than that, it was obvious that this was a challenging property being naturally prone to condensation forming. There were a lot of environmental factors working against the occupants in this building. The orientation and layout of the flat, the lack of any outdoor space and reluctance to open windows regularly all led to a high propensity for condensation formation. They do still have to live in the flat after all and only so much can be changed in a building!

I advised them to fit a positive pressure ventilation system. This works the opposite way to an extractor fan and creates a constant 'trickle' air change without needing mechanical extraction or windows to be left open. The systems run constantly and in this case the installation made a big difference to the condensation formation in the flat. The ventilation system helped to reduce the levels of moisture vapour being built up by allowing a flow of air change to outside.

This, coupled with the occupants being more careful and educated about how to help themselves with condensation control, meant that the condensation at this flat was significantly reduced.

The lessons:

When you see a damp patch, don't always assume that there is a leak from outside.

You need to look inside the property as well as outside to help understand the problem and design a solution.

All of us need to be more aware of how to control condensation in properties. In extreme cases condensation can cause a raft of health issues and make a property uninhabitable. Nowadays we construct our houses with airtight technology and rely entirely on natural and mechanical means of ventilation to help prevent condensation forming.

Perhaps there is a lesson here from the past. Think of your Victorian mid terrace house 'as built'. That would have had draughty sash windows and open fireplaces and tall flues in most rooms. The effect would have been a very high degree of ventilation and air change from the property. Over the years, very commonly, those windows are replaced with sealed double-glazed units and the fireplaces are blocked up. Perhaps we should not be so surprised to find that condensation is something which seems to affect many properties.

The Valentine's Day Massacre

By Angelos Sanders

Similar to how all good stories begin, it was a nice quiet evening on Valentine's Day. I was all set to relax and go on a nice Valentine's date. The restaurant table and cinema tickets were all booked. It had been a long day at the office and I had just pulled up outside my home, tired but excited for the evening.

I was about to turn off the car ignition when a call came through from a tenant called Juliet who was living in a 3-bedroom shared house. She was in hysterics saying that her housemate Romeo was trying to break down the door. I suggested keeping her door locked (the door was a fire door so it was strong and heavy and the person trying to break through would likely break their hand before getting in) and wait until I had arrived. I raced down there to see what was going on as I have experience with diffusing tricky situations (the trickier situation could be explaining to my girlfriend that I might have to cancel our date and then I would need to lock myself away as well).

I entered the building and all was quiet, which was a bit weird considering the pandemonium I just heard over the phone. I went straight upstairs to see Juliet and asked her what had happened? She explained that she had wanted to use the washing machine and Romeo's underwear was still in there. She felt great annoyance at this and proceeded to empty the contents of the washing machine onto the dining table to make a point to him. Romeo walked in and was mortified to see his underwear on display for all to see. He became angry and confronted her, hit her and then all hell broke loose.

Romeo retired to his bedroom and Juliet retired to her room and the other housemate was dumbfounded, asking himself what had just happened?

Romeo was very upset by all that had happened and was in tears. I listened to his side of the story and explained that although he might have felt justified, he cannot hit people and that Juliet had every right to report this to the Police. He understood this and really wanted a chance to apologise for his behaviour. I said to stay there and I would go and speak with Juliet and listen to her side of the story and see what she wanted to do.

Juliet was in her room and let me sit down and I listened to her account, which was similar to Romeos. She had calmed down and was willing to hear out Romeo. Romeo came upstairs and joined me in the bedroom – not quite the right girl's bedroom that I wanted to be in that evening, but there I was nonetheless acting as the United Nations. Romeo entered the room sheepishly and got on one knee and began to apologise. He seemed very sincere and afterwards, the two of them agreed to put the incident behind them and they hugged it out. Peace had been achieved and my work was done.

After the Valentine's Day massacre, both Romeo and Juliet actually became quite good friends by the end of the tenancy.

Lessons learnt:

- Encourage tenants to address any tensions early on before they explode and immediately deal with tenant safety issues.

Poo Girl

By Angelos Sanders

Warning: if you have a weak stomach or are about to eat, this story is probably not for you.

My day started out as any normal morning, the sun was shining and the birds were singing; nothing prepared me for what I was about to experience.

I received a phone call from a worried tenant who was concerned that her fellow housemate had returned from a very rough night out and was not responding to anyone's calls to see if she was well. The tenants asked me to come to the house straight away and check on what had happened and see if she was still alive. I drove there wanting to gauge what exactly was going on and hopefully see that nothing bad had happened to her.

I walked upstairs and my senses were assaulted by a strong smell of excrement.

I walked to her front door and I noticed poo had been smeared all over the door handle. There are times as a property investor when you sometimes wonder whether all this is worth it. This was definitely one of those days.

I knocked on her door and there was no response. I shouted out to her and she slowly awoke. Thankfully she was still responsive. I asked her to open the door, which she eventually did and then my second poo surprise was revealed.

I want you to imagine the arc that a door opens with. She swung the door open and before I could say or do anything, I looked down and there was diarrhoea on the carpet behind the door. She swung the door wide open and had smeared the diarrhoea in a nice arc shape following the path of the door. This was later nicknamed as the "arc of poo." And who said that investing in property isn't glamorous?

Trying to hold back my disgust and anger, I asked her "what happened?"

She explained to me what had happened and how she got herself into such a sorry state. She had been out partying that night and maybe had had a few interesting substances. She had lost control of her bowels on her way home and then raced home holding her shorts up, keeping the contents within until she had to open her door, which led to her smearing the handle and vacating her shorts on entry. Without thinking or probably being unaware of just what a sorry state she was in, she then went straight to bed.

Needless to say, she paid for a professional clean and moderated her evenings out for the rest of the tenancy.

Lessons learnt:

- Respond quickly to anyone's concerns regarding tenant safety.
- Perhaps some chess and a nice cup of hot chocolate could be substituted occasionally for a crazy night out?

House of Grime and Poo

By Vicki Wusche

Sourcing and buying a property is the start of a long relationship with your investment and the tenants that come with it.

Anyone considering or running an HMO (House of Multiple Occupation) strategy always has my admiration as there are many more tenants under one roof and all that entails. That is not to say that single family lets can be any easier.

So apart from the weed farms, which sadly pay really well and on time, and the tenants who don't pay, on time or at all – the most annoying we have had, have been the dirty tenants. Our worst to date has been "Dirty Diana"!

Dirty Diana came as a private tenant with her partner and four children. A couple of years into the tenancy the relationship broke down and Diana went on to benefits. From an income perspective the rent was still the same and the letting agent continued to carry out annual inspections as the tenant had been in place a long while.

Somewhere between her partner moving out and our next inspection Diana evolved or devolved should I say! To summarise, my letting agent worked with Diana for two years – literally buying cleaning products and teaching her to clean and then agreeing cleaning tasks that Diana was to complete before the next visit in four weeks' time – all to no real avail. While the rent was still being paid - our attention shifted towards the wellbeing of the children. The agent and I had numerous conversations about what to do next – whether to evict or intervene; it was a challenging position to be in. In the end, I agreed that my letting agent should start to work with social services and the school to get help for the family. Nothing made any difference.

In the end after working in partnership with the tenant for a further two years, I had to call time on the tenancy. I really did not want to evict a tenant who was paying her rent, but more importantly I did not want to disrupt the children. In the end health and safety was of too great a concern.

The cooker, clogged with grease, stopped working and there was no alternative, but to replace it. That was ultimately what led to the eviction process because there was simply no way a builder or electrician could work safely in the house.

My biggest regret after the eviction, of course, was not taking more pictures – no words can express the mess or the smell. We found used, almost fossilised, nappies under the mother's bed – the youngest child was five! The children's bedroom carpet was their night-time toilet and we had to replace the floorboards to get rid of the smell.

This story was sad, depressing even, but recoverable had she had family support and we could have ensured the children's safety.

HMO Horror

By Steve Dorrans

Way back in 2013 I had almost zero experience in the property business, other than a few lodgers in a house I had owned back in the late 90s. Still, that technically meant I had some HMO (House in Multiple Occupation) letting experience, so it was fitting that I had decided the best route into the property business was via a rent-to-rent HMO business.

I had spent several months learning about the property business, going to networking meetings, and attending training courses.

I had done my market research, worked out the precise area to find properties, what size of houses and rooms I needed, written a business plan and educated myself on the local planning and licensing laws. I was pretty much out of ways to procrastinate (sorry, educate myself) and it was finally time to pull the trigger and do some deals. Three months (and an uncomfortably large number of viewings) later, I was the proud owner of a property rental contract which permitted me to redecorate, fit fire doors and alarms and rent the rooms out to young professionals.

And so began my actual education about the world of HMO management. I would eventually end up with 84 tenants to look after, and almost as many horror stories about all the HMO problems that somehow never made their way into the property training courses.

But let's start with the very first one. My first HMO refurbishment went really well, finished on time and only *slightly* over budget. It was a four bed, two-bathroom house which I converted into a five bed by turning the living room/dining room into a fifth extra-large room and I got the all clear from the local Council to get it licensed and rented out with no problems – all that training had paid for itself already!

I advertised the rooms on Easyroommate and Spareroom with an open house viewing booked for the Saturday. Two enterprising individuals showed up on the Friday afternoon asking for an early viewing so I had two rooms rented out before the open house and the other three were all taken before lunchtime on Saturday. This room rental business was easy! My family, who had showed up to visit (and presumably to check that the house was real) and were suitably impressed. Unsurprisingly, the first room to rent was the top floor room which had the ensuite shower room and toilet.

One of the Friday arrivals was a solicitor (Dromio). Everything was going swimmingly well. The housemates were getting on well and I had a good relationship with the landlords who had offered me a second house in the same street and potentially a third when it came up for contract renewal.

Then I got a phone call from one of the housemates. They hadn't seen Dromio for a few days and there was an odd smell coming down the stairs from his top floor room. It was just before Easter weekend so I thought Dromio might have simply gone away for the weekend. I called his mobile several times but could only get voicemail. However one thing was nagging at the back of my mind; what could the odd smell be? We were in the middle of a period of unseasonably hot weather and I started to wonder what the smell of a decomposing body was like. I was also acutely aware from talking to landlords at training courses and networking meetings groups of the horror stories of HMO tenants who had committed suicide in their rooms.

Still, I couldn't just go and enter his room without permission. Or could I? The room rental agreement had a provision that I could enter with no notice in an emergency. But was this an emergency? Being new to this, I had no experience to draw on and I was very keenly aware of landlords having legal issues with tenants after entering properties and being in breach of their contract. So, gradually filling with trepidation and dread, I decided to go up there and see what was going on. I thought maybe a witness might be good but in the interests of privacy but I didn't think it was appropriate to ask one of the other tenants. Instead I called my handyman, explained the situation, and asked if he could meet me there. Luckily, he agreed, so I jumped in the car and set off. As we climbed the stairs up to the top floor there was a definite smell of something rotten which got rapidly stronger as we approached the door. I really didn't want to turn that key and open it but at that point I had very little choice.

Inside the bathroom was a horrific scene and was worse than anything I had imagined in my head. It was made worse by the smell, which was truly indescribable. Suffice to say it churned my stomach and made me nauseous, forcing me to pull my t-shirt up over my nose and mouth to filter the worst away from my indignant nasal passages. I made a mental note that I mustn't touch anything in that revolting crime scene but that nonetheless I would have to take some pictures for evidence. At this point I was really glad I had brought a witness but it was clear that my handyman would be unable to help with this problem, apart from maybe opening a window to let some fresh air in. Still, at least no-one was dead and I wasn't going to have to call the Police. There is a scene in the 1996 movie Trainspotting in which Ewan McGregor's character Renton dashes into "the worst toilet in Scotland" to relieve his diarrhoea and ends up diving into it to recover his lost opiate suppositories. The British movie going public was famously nauseated by the faeces-smeared toilet, walls and floors and the sight of Renton diving headfirst into the toilet bowl. The scene in front of me was worse for two reasons:

Firstly, the toilet stall in Trainspotting didn't have a shower in it, with the shower tray full to the brim and overflowing, with stinking brown water and floating pieces of poop dropping onto the floor. Secondly, watching Trainspotting (on my TV at least) there was absolutely no smell. Standing on the threshold of that bathroom scene the stench was so strong it almost had its own personality, and an unfortunately clingy one at that. I could definitely imagine it following me all the way home that night.

It was pretty clear what had happened. The ensuite toilet had a Saniflo macerator and pump attached to a small outflow pipe. During the check-in process Dromio and I had a lengthy conversation about the Saniflo unit and the inevitable consequences of flushing anything other than human waste and toilet paper down the toilet bowl. He had assured me he understood and that he would absolutely follow the rules. And yet, and yet and yet...

On top of the cistern and directly underneath the laminated warning sign about exactly what could be flushed, was a half-empty pack of "non-flushable" baby wipes. It wasn't going to take a Sherlock Holmes degree of deductive brilliance to work out what had happened here and just before Easter weekend. Quite literally the worst time to call out a tradesman to fix something like this. My handyman excused himself by making some retching noises, hand over mouth, and pointing to the door. I nodded and followed him to the welcome relief of the stairwell. It turned out he was trying to explain that having just seen this grotesque mess under his feet, it was also simultaneously way over his head. I thanked him for his help and called my plumber to explain the problem and ask him for help.

"Oh, I don't deal with Saniflo mate, you're going to need a proper Saniflo engineer for that," he said. I couldn't blame him for not wanting to get involved, I certainly didn't want to be. Anyway, he helpfully gave me the number of someone who could help and I rang it several times with no response. I could feel anxiety rising in the back of my throat. Or possibly vomit. After all these years my memories are a bit hazy, like the air in the ensuite bathroom that day. This was getting serious.

Then my phone rang. It was Dromio.

"Hi, sorry I missed your call. I'm on my way up to Scotland for the weekend but I was going to call you because the toilet in my bathroom doesn't seem to be flushing properly." You could say that again. "I was hoping you could get it fixed before I come back on Monday."

There is a principle trial lawyers like to quote "Never ask a question in court which you don't already know the correct answer to." This seemed like a good time to make use of it.

“When you say it’s not flushing properly, what do you mean?” I asked.

“Well, the water doesn’t seem to be going down quickly. It’s just not flushing properly” he replied.“Did you flush anything down that you shouldn’t have? You know, like we talked about when you moved in?” I asked.

“No, of course not” He replied.

“That’s weird” I said. “How long has it been like that for?”

“A couple of days.” I felt my eyes rolling and jaw dropping. “I’ve just been really busy and never got round to calling you.”

“OK.” I said. “Are you OK with me going in there without you to check it out?”

“Of course, thank you.” he replied. “I really appreciate your help.”

I wished him an enjoyable weekend and, silently in my head, thanked him for the one he had just saddled me with.

A couple more fruitless rings to the Saniflo engineer’s phone and I decided he had probably knocked off for the weekend. It was time to get on Google and search for a new one.

Two fruitless attempts at getting through to a human later, I was getting increasingly anxious. It was third time lucky though, a wonderful chap actually answered his phone. Result!

I explained the problem to him and he had clearly heard it all before. He asked me the model number of the Saniflo unit and when I found it and told him, he did that tradesman thing we have all learned to dread, sucking the air in through his teeth and pausing.

“Really? They aren’t used very often so I probably won’t have parts for that one. I can get them, but it might take a few days. I can be there Tuesday if that’s any good?”

Five days of festering, foul human waste smell drifting through my shiny new HMO and it's four other residents' nostrils. This was not appealing. I decided to abandon dignity and start begging.

Luckily, he was a thoroughly decent bloke. He absolutely would not be persuaded to come out on Good Friday but very kindly agreed to come up on the Saturday morning.

I called Dromio to update him and he was very pleased. I also took the opportunity to remind him that he was financially responsible for any damage caused by flushing inappropriate items down the toilet and explained that I had taken a picture of the half empty packet of baby wipes on top of the cistern. "Really?" he said, doing quite a good job of sounding amazed. "They must be my girlfriends. She occasionally stays with me and must have left them there."

My lawyer brain wondered why he sounded surprised. Presumably if his girlfriend habitually brought baby wipes, he would have noticed them sitting on his toilet? Maybe it was because she had forensically removed all other traces of ever having been in either the bathroom or the bedroom and he couldn't believe she had left this one irrefutable piece of evidence of her existence.

Anyway, I would never be able to figure out that little pickle, so I took the opportunity to remind him that his agreement said he was responsible for any damage caused by his guests. If the engineer did find baby wipes blocking the Saniflo, Dromio would be responsible. If it was a mechanical or electrical fault, I would of course pick up the tab for him. He agreed, quickly and cheerfully enough that I started to doubt myself if we would find baby wipes in there after all.

Next job, inform the other tenants of what was happening without appearing to attach any blame to Dromio. After all, we never want disharmony in our HMOs, all best friends is the ideal way forwards. Luckily for me, with the bathroom door closed and the bedroom window open, the smell in the rest of the house had dissipated (or I had gotten far too used to it). In addition, because it was a bank holiday weekend, the weather was turning a bit chillier and cloudier, which would presumably slow down the decomposition a bit until we had got everything drained down and cleaned. I sent the other housemates an email and a text message to explain there was a blocked drain in Dromio's bathroom and that I had managed to get a plumber out for Saturday. None of the other housemates raised it with me again after that, so I guess either they didn't notice it much or it didn't really affect them. Always try to be up front and ahead with communication when you are managing problems; tenants appreciate that much, much more than being kept in the dark and having to chase you for information.

Saturday morning rolled around. I was kind of dreading it because of the nausea of my first visit and briefly wondered where I could get a 17th Century plague doctor mask to help me cope. Eventually I had to stop being ridiculous and went back to the crime scene to let the plumber in and (hopefully not have to) help him out.

He was a cheerful chap who took everything in his stride and was very pleasant to be around. That is, apart from the sucking air in through his teeth thing, which he immediately did again when he saw the Saniflo. "Why on Earth have they wedged it in behind the bowl like that?" he said. "There's no way I can get in there and clean it out without removing the toilet first."

It was quite a small ensuite shower room and to save space the designers had used a slim Saniflo unit and had both cleverly and stupidly managed to fit the toilet over it so that it was near-impossible to work with before using some strong adhesive to glue the toilet bowl to the floor.

It was heart sink time again. "Seriously?" I asked, "But you can still do it, right?"

"Sure, he said. But there's a real chance that I'll crack the toilet bowl when I remove it because of the way they have glued it in there. I'm going to need a backup bowl just in case and I'll need permission from your landlords to do the work as well. For now, I'll drain this lot down", he said, gesturing to the toilet bowl and shower tray, "and I'll come back when I have everything I need. Is next Thursday all right with you?"

It really wasn't, given that Dromio was back on Monday, but what else could I do? The plumber drained down the mess at hand into the main bathroom's toilet, using a siphon system and a very long hose. If you're wondering, I'm pretty sure he wasn't down there sucking on the hose to get it started, like you might if you were siphoning petrol from a car, but honestly, I wasn't there to check.

Time for some more customer service.

I had to call Dromio and give him the good news/bad news. So, I put my smiley face on and dialled his number. It's fair to say he was not happy at all that it wasn't going to be fixed before he got back and he was adamant he couldn't stay in his bedroom until it was. It was time for some home truths at this point.

"I'm really sorry Dromio and I don't want to have to come back to this next week either but what can I do? The day before Easter weekend is literally the worst time to call me about something like this and, to be honest, I'm amazed I managed to get someone out to start the job on a Saturday. If you had called me a couple of days earlier, we might have had a chance of dealing with it before the weekend but we are where we are and rest assured, I'm doing everything I can to sort it out as fast as I can."

Dromio was a really nice guy at heart and he calmed down a bit and apologised. I suggested he might want to stay with his girlfriend for a couple of nights while he was waiting but he said that wouldn't be possible. That seemed reasonable enough but if he was angling for me to put him up in a hotel or something, he was sorely disappointed. I did however point out that there was low-cost B&B nearby and offered to reimburse him for his stay there if it turned out that it wasn't baby wipes blocking the Saniflo. I finished off by messaging the other tenants with an update and letting them know the plumber and I would be back Thursday.

Thursday arrived. When the plumber and I arrived, Dromio wasn't in his room, although he had clearly been sleeping there. Perhaps he wasn't confident in his insistence that there were no baby wipes in the Saniflo? At least, not enough to gamble the cost of three nights in a B&B.

Rightly so, as it turned out. The plumber pulled them out with a pair of long nosed pliers and waved them, a little unnecessarily I think, in front of my face. Still, I was grateful to him for finding them and took a couple of pictures for the evidence pile. He was also wise enough to have brought a new toilet bowl because the old one did indeed crack slightly as it was being removed.

Still, all's well that ends well, eh?

I documented it all and sent an invoice to Dromio for the cost of repairing the Saniflo. But would he pay for it? Well, it turns out he didn't have a huge amount of choice. Because I had set up all rental payments as direct debits rather than standing orders, I had the ability under the rent agreement to take the payment for the damage as an additional payment using the direct debit instruction. I gave him a week's notice of the payment to dispute it if he wished but being a decent, (largely) responsible human being, he didn't.

Which all goes to illuminate some lessons about HMO management. There's an oft-used phrase which applies in this instance "If you think education is expensive, try ignorance." I'm extremely grateful that I had some good education before I started. The courses I had been on and paid attention to had certainly saved me some heartache with this (potentially expensive) situation.

The main points for anyone starting down the HMO route are:

- Always fill your houses with decent, honest people. Always do a telephone interview and meet them in person to get a feel for their personality. If you wouldn't feel comfortable letting them stay the night in your home, don't rent a room to them in your HMO.

- Always make sure you have a well-written, enforceable rental agreement with your tenant and make sure they sign and date it to say they have read and understood it. This will be your backup in the event of a dispute, not anything you merely say you talked about or agreed to.
- Always communicate with all your tenants if there is a problem in the house. Don't wait for them to chase you as you will build up much more faith and trust with them if you are open, honest and upfront.
- Saniflo units can be a nightmare if mistreated. Make sure it is specifically addressed in the contract, that there is a warning sign clearly posted above the toilet and that every tenant is asked to sign a check-in document to say that they have been told the rules for using it and the penalties for abusing it.
- Direct debit rents give you more control of charges and rent changes. Sure, they cost a couple of quid every month but you can easily price that in and it make administration a whole lot easier than standing orders, including getting an email notification every time one is cancelled (as opposed to having to wait until the monthly rent fails to arrive)
- Good tradespeople are worth their weight in gold. Look after them and always pay their invoices straight away to keep them happy with you.
- Always have a list of backup tradespeople for emergencies. Sometimes, even with the best intentions, the person you want to solve your problem may just not be able to get there in time.

Iron Man

By Angelos Sanders

Iron Man – the name evokes images of heroism but this next person was far from heroic and in fact it would be fair to say they bordered on being senseless.

On a scheduled routine inspection, there was a nice surprise for me in a shared house. Walking to the top of the stairs, on the landing was an iron shaped burn mark which burnt through the carpet, underlay and onto the wooden floorboard below. My first reaction was to question the sanity of people in general and how this could happen. There were two ironing boards in the house, so it was not through lack of equipment that they had to resort to using carpet instead.

I called a house meeting with all the tenants and asked who had done it. No-one knew who had burnt the carpet. "That is fine" I replied, "everyone can share the cost of replacing the carpet." All of a sudden, everyone turned to one tenant and I knew I had my culprit. I then gave them all a lecture on what materials burn and what do not. The things we sometimes have to do as investors! The carpet was replaced and Iron Man did not strike again.

Chapter 10

Landlords and Letting Agents

Bad Letting Agents

By Roy Inman

In the early days of my property investing career, I was working full time as a chef and I looked to leverage my time by using letting agents to manage my properties. Now a good letting agent, a really good letting agent, is worth their weight in gold. They have the potential to totally free you up from the everyday running and the worry of your property investments and leave you time to focus on enjoying your life and doing the things that you want to do, the things that you dreamed of doing when you became financially free. It can take away all of the legislation worries, the burden that is required with dealing with property management on a day-to-day basis, and it even allows you the time to continue to grow and build your portfolio, instead of getting sucked into dealing with problems.

The challenge I had whilst going through this process and learning about agents, good and bad, is the number of problems I had with bad agents. They varied from agent to agent from small independents up to even using a national agent. I had a national agent that was managing one of my properties, the tenant moved out and they were remarketing the property. The property was in great condition, six months later they still hadn't found me a tenant and I constantly had to chase them for updates, but also at this time I was still quite young and naive. I believed everything they said and trusted them because they were supposed to be the experts, or so I thought.

They should have been coming to me, giving me updates on where things were, what interest we'd had or any feedback. Alongside this, they should have been giving me advice on what could be done to let the property. A lot of the advice that you get from agents, can be very poor and this is because, in my opinion, they don't really know what they're doing. They just tell you to lower the rent and you'll get more interest. Nine times out of 10 they're the ones who have recommended that rental income in the first place, and they're now effectively saying they can't let it for that amount and that you need to drop the price and drop it again until you get a tenant interested.

They weren't giving any advice about the condition of the property. They weren't giving any feedback as to what was putting the tenants off applying for the property. Apparently, there were a lot of tenants interested in the property, viewing it, but no one was actually putting an application in.

Most agents just don't seem to give any advice or recommendation, and these specifically didn't. I found this across the board, that any advice or recommendation given was not on marketing the property to get more interest and using different marketing tactics, it was to just drop the rent. No advice around using professional photos or marketing and promoting the property in a different way. Maybe offering one-week free rent or the first months' rent half price, or potentially even a reduced deposit. You can now even look at going down the avenue of a deposit replacement scheme to help fund, encourage and entice potential tenants and to make your property more appealing. But if you've got a great property, in a good location, at the right price, there shouldn't be any problems whatsoever in renting it.

Now another agent, this time a small independent that I had problems with, was managing my property and it all seemed great. Everything was going well and they started off doing a great job, they found a good tenant pretty quickly. Well, it seemed like a really good tenant. After a number of months, I think it was about four or five months, I kept getting excuses about the rent being paid across. They were either waiting for it from the tenant or they'd been away or they'd just been busy and they'd get right on to it. I then struggled to get hold of them and when I did, I got different excuses again and again, and this then built up and built up. Obviously, you chase and you chase, you try and find out what's going on. But if you can't get hold of them, you can't speak to them, it's very difficult to find out what is happening.

I even went to their office and that was closed. I couldn't speak to them that way and in the end, I ended up having to go to see the tenants and speak to them face to face to find out what was going on. The agent themselves ended up disappearing and running off with £3,450 of the rent that I should have received. Shortly after that maybe two or three weeks, I went to a local landlord Council meeting. The group was like a landlord forum, there were about 55 of us there and it transpired that the Council were fully aware of the agent in question and that this was not the first time they had taken rent from tenants and not passed it onto the relevant landlord.

The Council knew about it but weren't really that interested in doing anything. The agent ended up disappearing out of the country and I lost that money. There was nothing that I could do. Now things have moved on and you've got client money protection which all agents must be registered with, client money protection then gives landlords like you the reassurance and protection I never had. They should also have a client account that is managed correctly and monitored. These are just a couple of the issues I've been through over the years. And, like I say, having a great agent looking after your investments, is something that is worth its weight in gold - it really is.

As more and more of these problems came about with agents (don't get me wrong, I did have some good agents as well) I got to a point where I made the decision, enough was enough, and that led me to bringing the management of nearly all my portfolio in house.

After some major challenges managing the properties myself that cost me a lot of money and is a whole other story, I set up all the systems and processes to run and manage the properties in the portfolio. I wanted to manage them in the way that I felt that it should be from both an investor perspective and an agent's point of view combined. I created all that was needed to make sure that things were running in, not only the most efficient way, but the best way to look after the property and the tenants as well.

Then, as that progressed, other landlords I knew started to see how well things were running and how the occupancy level was. The landlords and investors started asking me to manage their properties as well. Sure Move, my letting and property management agency was born and grew from there.

There are many other stories of landlords who have moved their property management to us as well as they've had similar experiences with agents. We were managing some property for one landlord, who then recommended us to another landlord as they were having problems with their current agent. After taking on one of their HMOs, which we finished off overseeing the refurbishment, we then dressed the property, organized professional photography, and let the rooms with ease. We went on to continue to manage it. They were so impressed with how well things had worked compared to all their previous experiences.

Due to the levels of communication, the knowledge, and the efficiency, we had dealt with their HMO, they decided to transfer all of their properties to us to manage. Now just before transferring them to us, they realised that the agent that they were currently with had also been way overcharging them for maintenance and we are not talking a little bit because they used very expensive contractors. They were absolutely ripping them off. I had a look at some of the information and quotes that were sent across from the agent and they'd been quoted and charged three and a half times more than what the job should have been. That's 300% over what it should have cost! I was shocked and disgusted that there are agents that do that. When you've got a job that should cost around £110 and they were quoted £395 to do that job. I just couldn't get my head around it; I was speechless and that doesn't happen very often. I was just glad we could help them and that they now had and agent they could trust.

Another landlord had bought a property off plan over 10 years before we managed their property and they'd never seen it. I'm not sure how the property was acquired, whether it was direct or through an investment company. They then trusted the managing agent that they were working with to look after it for the 10 years that they'd owned it and never seen it. They'd had different tenants move in and out, it got to a point where a tenant had moved out and the agent had not let the property for over four months. At this point the landlord, living miles away, was very concerned about what was going on. They contacted us, we had a conversation with them and we really couldn't see why the property hadn't been let within such a long period of time.

So we conducted an inspection and gave a full, honest feedback report and it basically came to light that the agent had not undertaken any routine maintenance over the last 10 years and the property was an absolute mess. We're not even sure if they even conducted a move out when the tenant moved out or if there had even been any viewings. The walls were really, really dirty, horribly dirty and damaged. The carpets were worn and torn in some areas. The kitchen cupboard doors and laminate for the doors was peeling off and the property as a whole was just filthy. We spoke to the landlord, discussed all this with them and explained that this was one of the reasons why they hadn't had any applications. Speaking to the landlord, we found that the agent had not informed the landlord of any of this and was not giving them any advice on what they needed to do to let the property. In the time period that the property had sat empty, the landlord had lost nearly £5,500 in lost rent.

On top of the financial loss, was all the work that needed to be done and they'd returned the full deposit back to the previous tenant and who knows how much of the damage was caused by them. Now we find that this is actually a common theme that we come across with a lot of the landlords who move to us and it seems that the agents just don't seem to care. They don't seem to understand it, from an actual landlord investor point of view because most agents aren't landlords and investors themselves. They don't have their own properties that they look after or know what it's like to have an investment of that value. They just don't seem to fully grasp and understand that they are managing someone's investment. It's possibly their pension, their inheritance to pass onto their children, the legacy that they're leaving behind. It's their livelihood in the long run, if not currently. And because of that, they don't understand the commercial cost implications to the landlord or investor when a property is sat empty and how much of an impact voids have on that profit margin.

It's crazy when you have a conversation with an agent and find that actually their knowledge and their experience is so lacking in the understanding of what it is like being an investor and what it means to actually have an investment property. Sometimes they just don't seem to have the knowledge, experience, or drive to want to solve the problem. Sometimes they're an agent who is trying to operate with cheap fees, this is a big one that we come across a lot, and they don't have the physical staff and resources to be able to deliver on the service that they should be providing. We had another landlord recently who had a prime example of this when they had their newly refurbished, beautiful five bed HMO property on the market with an agent for over three months and they hadn't even filled one room in the entire property.

The property was newly converted and had been dressed beautifully. There was absolutely no reason why it shouldn't have been filled. When we dug into it and got to the crux of it, the agent didn't know the market in that area. We don't really think they specialised in professional HMO management from what we looked at, and they just thought they could do it and that it was the same as buy-to-let management, which it definitely isn't! They had terrible marketing photos, an awful description of the property and they'd also overpriced the rooms to get the business from the landlord, along with offering low fees.

For the months that the property was empty, in total, across all of the rooms, this cost the landlord over £6,500 in lost rental income. In that period, the entire property should have been let! The landlord transferred the property to us. All the frameworks, knowledge and fine-tuned processes that we have put in place over the last 19 and a half years of me investing in property, we then applied to this property and we filled four out of the five rooms in less than three weeks, just by knowing what the problems were and looking after the landlord's investment. As I'm sure you can imagine, they are very, very happy now that the property is let. It's so important to make sure that you've got a good agent to look after your property, give you and your tenants' peace of mind, and allow you to enjoy your life and protect your investment.

Bad Landlords

By Roy Inman

Landlords are sometimes no angels and it's not always the tenant or agents fault. I've been involved with property for nearly 20 years, as an investor and managing agent, and over the years I have had experiences with agents who managed my properties in the early days, tenants when managing my own properties and landlords when managing properties for them.

As a landlord/investor myself, I have come to the realisation that sometimes I can be part of the problem and landlords need to take responsibility and an understanding that this is the case. This then allows their agent to be able to do their job properly if they are using one. If you don't take that responsibility and don't do the things that you need to do, then sometimes it can make it very difficult for your agent and it may be your fault.

I'll give you some examples of some of the landlord challenges that we've had over the years and hopefully maybe you can make sure that you're not a landlord like this.

We had a landlord who had owned a property for 10 years, had never seen it, the agent they were using had never done any routine maintenance and it had been empty for over four months. We conducted a thorough inspection of the property and gave them a full review of recommendations to bring the property up to a lettable condition along with a marketing proposal. We arranged for quotes and project managed the work through to completion.

We also marketed the property and found a tenant within two weeks of the works being completed who was also paying 10% over market rent. What we then found was that due to the previous agent not conducting any routine maintenance work (letting the property condition deteriorate over the years) the landlords expectation (this was their only buy to let property) was that you didn't ever have to do routine maintenance and it is not a cost you have to account for. Their belief now, was that between buying it off plan, new build, 10 years ago and up until now they hadn't had this cost, and so they wouldn't have it for the next 10 years either. Now that's not the reality of property investment, you're never going to have that happen even if everything has been completely stripped back to brick and all redone anew.

Over the years you're going to have some maintenance and wear and tear over the course of a tenancy and years of having the property. But the landlord decided to start refusing for works to be done, to the point of actually leaving the tenants with appliances that had been supplied in the property that weren't working. Now this starts to cause all number of problems as it creates liability under breaches of legislation under the Housing Act, for both themselves and us, which left us no choice but to cancel our management contract because they were refusing to have any work done to the property. What they then did is moved to a cheap agent who is probably going to repeat the same experience he had previously had and ended up costing even more in lost rent and possible legal action against them if he doesn't do required maintenance and conform to legislation.

Now, one thing I learned growing up is that you can't have the best for the cheapest price. If you go for cheap, it usually breaks quicker or it's just not as good quality. Any service won't be great and a business just can't make the best product and be the cheapest price as they won't last very long. The margin just isn't there, if they cut the price then they have to cut the quality to stay in business. They have to source cheaper materials and/or cheaper labour and the same applies for service businesses. You can't deliver the best service if the fees you charge don't allow you to. You're just trying to be cheap. You don't have the staff or the resources to be able to deliver that level of service.

Now you've probably heard the saying, "you get what you pay for." I also learned a great saying from a very good friend of mine, and that it's as simple as, "you buy cheap, you buy twice." It's one of the truest sayings I have ever come across and applies to both physical products and services. You just end up having to pay out again for the same product or service because it breaks or the service you get just isn't up to scratch. Remember that when you're choosing your next agent, you get what you pay for and if you buy cheap, you'll pay twice.

I just want to share one more landlord challenge with you as I could tell you stories for days. One great landlord, who's a really nice person, likes to work with investors who lend them money to purchase the property and refurbish it. This is a great way to build a portfolio if done correctly and helps you leverage your own money as well as potentially being able to buy more properties at the same time, or even get started if you don't have much or any money of your own. What they have a tendency to do is to overstretch themselves potentially causing cash flow issues, which puts them under pressure. A little pressure is a good thing until it moves you into some area of desperation. They have a mixture of single buy-to-lets and HMOs and when it comes to filling the rooms or the property, they need it filled yesterday, they start to get really desperate and then advertise the property themselves along with us as agents. They then conduct a viewing usually at the weekend without informing us.

Monday morning arrives and we are informed that they have conducted a viewing over the weekend, moved the tenant in the same day with no references, no credit or background checks at all and sometimes without even taking any deposit upfront. They've agreed a payment plan to pay the deposit over a number of weeks, which is generally all verbal with the tenant and only taking a week's rent up front.

Apart from one week's rent, they have nothing else as protection, then when it doesn't all work out and a few months later the tenant stops paying their agreed deposit, and possibly the rent as well they don't understand why it's all gone wrong and what the issue is. They've even had situations where they've moved tenants in without even issuing all of the relevant documentation to make sure they're fully legal and compliant under the Deregulation Act, leaving themselves open to not being able to issue a Section 21 notice and end the tenancy if they wanted to.

This is all because they don't know what they're doing when it comes to property and lettings management. The legislation and the law along with the potential liability and fines that they could be very easily caught with and over the last 10 years this area of compliance has tripled, if not quadrupled compared to before and there are so many areas that can go wrong.

They are just focusing on the short-term gain of getting someone in and getting some rent due to the cash flow issues and hope that will sort the problem. Forgetting about the potential medium to long term problems that could easily be 10 times worse with the build-up of rent arrears, potential fines and if you get it really wrong, imprisonment.

I know another landlord who owns five properties and self manages, I've had conversations with him over the years and he has admitted point blank to me that he's not issued all the correct documentation when moving his tenants in and he hadn't even heard of over half of them. If he ever needed to evict the tenants, he would struggle because he didn't issue the correct paperwork and it could cost him thousands to sort the problem out.

Getting The Name Right

By Phil Oke

Marcus Aemilius Lepidus (Marcus for short) had a portfolio of properties – some in his personal name, and some in the name of the limited company which he subsequently set up – Marcus Aemilius Lepidus Company (referred to as Marcus's Company for the rest of this story.)

In this case, Marcus' Company had bought a property back in 2002 and it was registered as the owner at Land Registry. However, when the tenancy was granted a few months later, his managing agent incorrectly recorded Marcus as Landlord on the tenancy agreement.

The agent had also served a Section 21 possession notice which had expired and the tenants had not moved out so a possession order was required. The name given on the notice as landlord was Marcus.

As will be appreciated, Marcus (the individual), and Marcus's Company (the company), were separate legal entities and so Marcus had no power in law to grant the tenancy since he was not the owner of the property. Given the legal mix up, which I explained to Marcus, I advised that there was a risk that the court might not grant a possession order to the company.

I was instructed to "give it a go" and submit an application to the court which I duly did.

The tenants were an elderly couple with health issues and the husband was a particularly awkward individual. A very lengthy and rambling Defence was submitted, raising a number of issues, including alleged discrimination under the Equality Act 2010 and, more significantly, what I labelled the "landlord name issue." On my recommendation, we sought advice from a local barrister specialising in Housing Law whom I have used in the past in the more complex cases I have handled, as a "second pair of eyes". He advised that the claim for possession could succeed, but there was no guarantee that it would. Instead, he recommended, sensibly, that Marcus's Company should discontinue the court proceedings and start again, with not just one but two notices – one on behalf of the company, and one on behalf of Marcus.

Marcus agreed and fresh notices were served. However, the tenants did not move out and so court proceedings had to be instituted, with a fresh application for a possession order brought in the names of both Marcus personally and the company Marcus's Company.

As with the previous case, a lengthy Defence was filed, with the tenants still contesting the claim to possession. The case proceeded to a hearing where the Judge, rightly, granted Marcus's Company a possession order. Although he also ordered the tenants to pay a sum of money towards Marcus's Company's costs, they had no assets and no income beyond state pensions so Marcus's Company had to foot their entire legal bill. The tenants eventually left the property a few days before being ordered to do so by the court.

With the increasing trend over recent years – especially for tax reasons – for landlords to create limited companies to purchase and own properties, rather than them personally, it is vitally important that where landlords and agents check that names marry up and that the correct name of the landlord is recorded on the tenancy agreement. The failure to do so in this case meant that it took a lot longer than normal to evict the tenant and it cost the landlord significantly more in legal costs.

The Importance of Having a Written Tenancy Agreement and Taking Action on Rent Arrears

By Phil Oke

Grumio and the tenant knew each other socially. The tenant asked if she could rent his property which Grumio agreed to. They agreed a rent but Grumio did not issue the tenant with a written tenancy agreement.

By the time I was instructed to evict the tenant the arrears were over £7,300. Grumio was insistent upon pursuing the tenant for payment.

As there was no written tenancy agreement, we use what is known as the "accelerated procedure" - where there is usually no court hearing - under Section 21. As this was still a valid Assured Shorthold Tenancy, albeit one created verbally, we could use the standard procedure – involving a hearing and thus costing more – to evict but we could not also claim the rent arrears under that process.

Given his instructions, I advised Grumio to proceed via Section 8 which we duly did. Unfortunately, the tenant, who bore real animosity towards Grumio, did not take kindly to receiving a possession notice, nor subsequently to being served with court papers. She filed a defence, and a counterclaim, making allegations of harassment and disrepair, and became increasingly hostile to both Grumio and myself.

In view of the defence and counterclaim, the court adjourned the initial hearing to another date when proper time could be allocated to deal with the case. Recognising the potential time and expense that would be involved in pursuing defended court proceedings, I advised Grumio to try to cut a deal, given also that the tenant was not working and, as such, it was unlikely that she would be able to recover the rent arrears. He instructed me to enter into negotiations whereby, in return for the tenant agreeing to drop her defence – and consenting to the grant of a possession order - and not pursue her allegations,

Grumio agreed not to pursue her for the rent arrears, which by then had increased further.

Fortunately, I was able to persuade the tenant to agree to a resolution of matters on this basis. The court was notified and the Judge granted the possession order which Grumio needed. That wasn't the end of it though. The tenant did not leave in accordance with the order and the court bailiff had to be appointed to evict her.

Had there been a written tenancy agreement, and Grumio not been insistent on also claiming the arrears, this case could have been concluded far quicker and at far less expense to him by using the Section 21 accelerated procedure.

Be Careful What You Say To Tenants

By Phil Oke

Ophelia was an elderly landlady. She rented out a house that she had inherited from her mother. The house needed to be sold to pay outstanding care home fees and she already had the property on the market for sale with a local estate agent. Fortunately for her, this was the case that came to me prior to the court decision in the *Monty Schooltz* case.

My instructions were to evict the tenants. Section 21 notices had to be used, but first I had to provide the tenants with copies of the Deregulation Act documents, which Ophelia had not done so when she set the tenancy up.

The tenants did not comply with the notice I served, so it proved necessary to issue court proceedings. Somewhat bizarrely, the tenants indicated that they had not been provided with the DA documentation. More significantly, they put forward a counterclaim seeking recovery of money they had spent on the property, which they alleged Ophelia had given her blessing to and had agreed to reimburse them for.

The amount claimed was in the region of £22,000. They were also claiming that in discussions they had had with her she had indicated that they could have first refusal when she put the property on the market. They also claimed that they had engaged the service of a mortgage broker as they were trying to raise the necessary finance to buy the property. This was all news to me so I questioned Ophelia about it. She told me that what the tenants were alleging was essentially correct.

Whilst I had no concerns about the validity of the notice, I did have concerns about how all this could muddy the waters and cause us problems. I was also mindful of the potential cost to Ophelia of dealing with the reimbursement claim, and the time involved. I took the view that a practical and pragmatic approach was required and that we should try to cut a deal with the tenants. Despite some initial reluctance on her part, Ophelia agreed to this recommendation. Consequently, discussions ensued, in tandem with preparing for the hearing. Unfortunately, these proved unsuccessful as the tenants would not accept the landlord's initial offer, or a subsequent improved offer.

On the day of the hearing the male tenant turned up at court and sought advice from the duty legal adviser. This was to prove helpful in the negotiations that followed as extensive negotiations resulted in a deal being reached, whereby the tenant agreed to drop the defence to the possession claim, and the counterclaim for reimbursement of the money spent on the house, in return for Ophelia agreeing to him and his family having longer to leave than the standard 14 day period and agreeing not to claim for payment of the legal costs she had incurred, or for the rent arrears that had begun to accrue by this stage. This deal was one which the advisor recommended to the tenant.

When we appeared before the Judge, the terms of settlement were approved and a possession order was granted, albeit that the tenants did not comply with it and the bailiff had to be appointed.

Whilst we got there in the end, this case cost Ophelia a significant amount in legal fees and caused her a huge amount of worry and stress.

Common features:

Each landlord shot themselves in the foot at the outset, none were professional landlords, none bar one used an agent to set the tenancy up and manage it for them, and in each case, we had a problematic/ awkward tenant who made trying to sort things out more difficult, more expensive, and more time-consuming.

The Great Furniture Dispute

By Verona Cocks

A landlord of a property let it fully furnished including some particular items which they had used themselves for years being a dining table and there was a built-in cupboard with featured doors. Although the tenancy provisions prevented alterations to fixtures without the permission of the landlord, the tenants took it upon themselves to remove the featured doors to the cupboards which had become damaged as a result and the other items, in particular the dining table which had been left for use, was heavily marked.

The landlord then wanted to sell the property and was prepared to do so with the tenants in situ, as an investment property. The tenants were not helpful with viewings, notwithstanding that the provisions of the tenancy required their cooperation and ultimately the buyer who came forward wanted vacant possession. The landlord, therefore, had to give notice but the tenants failed to leave on the expiry of that notice. Following further correspondence and the threat of possession proceedings the tenants did leave some months later, by which time the buyer had found another property. The landlord also tried to recover the loss to the damage of the items and the cupboard from the deposit through the tenancy deposit scheme but was unsuccessful.

The moral of the story is only leave furniture in the property which you do not care if it is damaged and make sure that the letting agents properly inspect the property which ought to pick up on unauthorised alterations to fixtures. In this case, the landlord eventually sold the property which provided a satisfactory conclusion.

Contracts And Trust - From Portfolio Landlord, To Exasperated Tenant

By Barbara Hosker

Though a contract might give you security, it is trust that ultimately gives you a successful business.

This enforced leisure time has created the opportunity for me to nosy into other property related businesses, most notably the TV programme 'Four in a Bed'. It is a competition for Bed & Breakfast owners who compete to see who has the best value B&B, featuring everything from stately homes to a tent in a field.

It's quite fascinating to observe different approaches to business. Apart from realising that some people's opinions on the standard of their property, can border on the delusional, to those whose egos are way higher than the standards of hosting skills.

Knowing full well they are entering a competition where standards of cleanliness is critical, there are rooms with tired, jaded, outdated mismatched furniture, filthy windows, decomposing pigeons on the windowsills, mice in the sofas, minging loo brushes, stained mattresses/bed linen, cobwebs that any horror movie would be proud of and enough spare 'curly hairs' to knit a rug.

What I find incredibly funny is that the standard of forensic investigation as to the cleanliness of other people's rooms on their visits. Beds are lifted, wardrobes pulled out, life and limbs are risked whilst abseiling down from the tops of curtain rails in the search for any single speck of dust or starter cobweb which, if found, is greeted with glee and an otherwise five-star establishment is then rated down to a score of 6/10.

Part of the problem here is that we don't 'see' our own stuff. So it's hard to spot when things aren't right, or what's being missed.

A great tip here is to take photographs of your rooms from different angles.

When you 'look' at a room, your brain filters things out whereas when you photograph it you suddenly see all sorts of things that need to be addressed.

The programme also shows the wildly different approaches that people take towards developing their businesses. From the ones in the power suits, with the 'bottom line' spreadsheets and the clear written business plan to the ones who just seem to have fallen into it letting out spare rooms in their home, with the owner's clothes still in the wardrobe.

Most people I know wouldn't buy a new car, without giving it a test run first.

When I had my properties, it never occurred to me for a moment to give any of them a test run, before I advertised them for rent. Now I'd heartily recommend it, especially testing out the shower (water pressure and drainage).

A property can look, at first glance and to all intents and purposes, to be lovely and habitable. However, the reality can be very different.

With my landlord head on, I'm looking for location and ROI (Return on Investment). I become a female Mr Spock and use logic-based decisions. With my tenant head on, it is emotional decisions, I'm looking for a certain 'lifestyle'.

Having 'test run' a number of rental properties now over the past few years, it's been a real eye opener.

I think the current score is that I could have been crushed, drowned, electrocuted, gassed, or blown up.

It's a real testament to the power of 'goodwill' when both the tenant and landlord become lasting friends, despite never meeting in real life and the tenant has moved on.

I think some landlords operate a system of what I loosely call 'benign neglect'. At the beginning of a tenancy a landlord and tenant sign a contract, an AST, it sets out what are rights and responsibilities of each party. It all seems to be pretty clear.

How and why do things go so badly wrong?

The contract doesn't necessarily give a full description of the underlying condition of the building. If a landlord knows that there are long standing problems - problems that aren't immediately obvious; things like temperamental drains, leaking roofs, windows that don't open/close properly, but fails to mention to the prospective tenant during the viewings, they potentially leave themselves open to all kinds of problems down the line.

This is where some knowledge about 'values and beliefs' is helpful. We can trip ourselves up when we say "well I wouldn't treat anyone that way" it's because we don't all operate under the same standards of behaviour.

One person's idea of cleaning the house might be another's perception of having OCD. One person's wildlife friendly garden is another person's nightmare if they like a 'not a dandelion' in sight space. This is where an inventory with photos stands the professional landlord in good stead as words can be misinterpreted. Those of you 'of a certain age' will well remember the hilarious estate agent descriptions of properties attempting to create a positive picture of a less than marketable property such as 'Bijou' or 'cosy' meaning 'tiny'.

As more and more legislation is foisted upon landlords, those who are full-time professionals are more likely to survive. The ones who just decide to self-manage renting out the old family home seem to come unstuck more often, especially if they have lived in the property themselves.

It is OK if it's your own home and you decide to take chances with safety. One would a think in this day and age, given the huge amount of property related info, that it would be almost impossible to find any landlords who haven't kept their gas/electrical safety certificates up to date, especially when it's possible to take out a contract with companies who undertake all management/repairs/certificates.

It is even scarier when you realise that there are still some who attempt DIY repairs to gas appliances.

It is also worth mentioning that insurance companies love their 'small print'. They know all about contract law. It is how they deny payment on claims. Landlords who cut corners on safety, risk losing everything, if they fail to follow industry legislation.

Legally as a Landlord I am obliged to ensure that any property I offer for rental is safe or I could face serious consequences. Huge fines, prison, or both so it is better to have a clear conscience and a good night's sleep.

The AST/contract sets out the rights and responsibilities but ultimately it comes down to trust.

- Trust that each party has been honest.
- Trust that each party will behave honourably.
- Trust that we will keep our written promises.
- Trust that the landlord will deal with any issues as they arise in a reasonable time.
- Trust that the tenant will genuinely, honestly care for the property.
- Sometimes, an AST/contract, in many ways, isn't worth the paper it's written on.

Goodwill and trust can make the difference between success or financial ruin and that makes them, therefore, priceless.

PART 4

PROPERTY BUSINESS NIGHTMARES

Introduction

Treating your property investments as a business will pay you dividends (no pun intended) in the end as you will have the necessary systems and processes in place to provide the best customer service for your customers and also will help to ensure the smooth running of your business.

There are many businesses that revolve around the world of property. For example, letting agents, brokers, insurance brokers, developers, sourcing financial services, consultancy; the list goes on.

With any business, you want to start as you mean to go on and that includes building your business with foundations of stone, rather than sand (pun definitely intended). There can be some real challenges when running a property business but similar to any other business, it is focussing on resolving these problems and implementing systems and processes to help prevent these things from happening again, is key to sustaining a long term and successful business.

As an aside, it is somewhat interesting to note that although the UK Government does not necessarily recognise private landlords as a business, it sure does know how to tax them like one. There are hundreds of rules and regulations that must be complied with in order to own, rent, manage, develop and source in the world of property. While we're on the subject of tax, the UK's tax laws have more pages than the complete works of Shakespeare!

No one can know everything. Therefore, it is especially important to make sure that you always get the best advice from the experts as possible.

Once you have built up your investments, it is vital to protect them with the right type and most comprehensive set of insurance policies. Managing risk is the most important thing.

This section has a series of stories with clear lessons that will be invaluable in your property business building.

The stories in the Business Nightmares section cover:

- Tax
- Finance
- Insurance
- Fire safety
- Property sourcing
- Business lessons

Chapter 11

Tax

HMRC Penalties and Disclosure

By Ashley Smith

This starts with a potential client meeting. The client had received an investigation letter from HMRC relating to his business. His mother had dealt with his accounts historically and it turned out there was a bank account he hadn't told her about. As the investigation progressed, we were surprised to find HMRC trying to assess him on property income as well. Following various discussions, we were surprised to uncover that his father had a property that had been let out for many years. On the sale of this property the father wanted to try and avoid any future Inheritance Tax and so, following a discussion in the pub, the new property was registered in the client's name. The father continued to receive the rent and therefore the client did not think anything of it.

Thankfully as we unravelled this from the client, we were able to advise his father and disclosed the information, avoiding any penalties. As the father had received the rent HMRC agreed, after many discussions, to treat this as his income, rather than that of the clients.

The moral of the story is that following advice given in the pub isn't necessarily the way to go.

The Deal That Never Was - Section 162 Incorporation Case

By Anonymous

We were contacted by one of the lending managers whom we work closely with, to assist a residential mortgage broker whose expertise lay elsewhere and who were struggling to place a complex and demanding Special Purpose Vehicle (SPV) funding requirement.

The client had been working with local brokers whom he knew and trusted, however they had never dealt with a case of this size or complexity nor, in-fact, had they ever placed a Ltd company mortgage before.

The requirement was a sizeable Section 162 incorporation case under case law set out by the Ramsay ruling. All personal mortgages needed to be settled, the portfolio would shift to Ltd company, and now limited company lenders would be required.

At the point we were brought in to assist as the previous broker had been working on the case for five months prior and had, at one point, felt that they had managed to solve the client's funding requirements, albeit in theory and there was a huge amount of hard work and practical task at hand.

However, they had not realised the lenders that they had approached, all wanted the same properties as security, which left a large chunk of properties which couldn't be lent upon which had meant the deal was currently unworkable from a finance perspective.

The deal comprised of hundreds of properties currently held in personal names with overall lending currently standing at £36.4m, with George Osborne's tax changes looming, this would kill the portfolios profitability at a damaging rate.

The clients owned a chunk of the properties that had been purchased historically on a sale and rent back basis being let back to the original owners of the properties. This was presenting as an issue as well as a number of properties locations meaning the lenders appetites were low.

Sale and rent back is a big lending hurdle for many lenders as the rights to reside usually override the lenders' rights. We have excellent connections with commercial lenders and were able to agree terms for this part of the deal requirement within 48 hours. With this part done we could then go through the remaining properties – street view, lenders requirements, rental calculations, exposure levels etc, all one by one and diligently place each case by referring the property to each lender for sight and prior approval. At this point we were only assisting the other broker and had no direct client contact.

Overall we would be using six lenders. From two of the main lenders we had secured agreement to refund fees to the tune of £29,556 from the standard fee tariffs. This isn't normally do-able but given that this was such a sizeable case, it had been something we had been able to negotiate. We had a very detailed Excel spreadsheet where we had done due diligence on every property across the portfolio to ensure that every case would complete as far as we could see, subject to the usual underwriting and valuations as expected.

The case was all or nothing, we could not incorporate some properties and not others, the guidance states that the whole business must be incorporated or nothing at all.

We worked alongside the clients brokers as mentioned, planning to package some of the deals for them but later to process all the deals with the other broker acting as an introducer.

Finally, having presented the case to the client via email, we arranged the all-important face to face meeting. We don't meet many of our clients, but with so many parties to tie together and with it being such an important and complex task, this was the way to go.

The client was suitably impressed with how the overall portfolio could be spilt across lenders to ensure the most cost-effective products across the board and also the savings we had made in fees. They were eager to go ahead, however there was one crucial part we couldn't help with and that was tax advice!

However, as brokers who have conducted tens of these types of incorporations over years, we knew that any new lenders would require to know who was imparting the tax advice and that it was good and proper, above board and correct. When we broached the conversation, we realised that there was no solid advice as yet and that they were currently seeking that approval. There was no point progressing any further until this was ticked off.

The unsolvable nightmare hit, the tax advice would not stand up to scrutiny given the client's circumstances, and the whole idea of incorporation had to be shelved.

The nightmare was now in wasted time, three months for the brokers who originally took the case and a week or so of tough, diligent work for us as specialist brokers.

Although the client would now have to think of another plan that would likely consist of planned disposal, we did avoid another nightmare, however. The clients could have spent considerable sums on valuation, conveyancing fees had this subject not been approached.

Worse still, they could have incorporated without proper advice only to find that an HMRC investigation ruled against them and the millions in SDLT and CGT fees they sought to mitigate would have become payable which would have been a total financial disaster.

What can we learn from this?

- Have great advisers around you with experience and know-how in complex affairs keeps your business robust and avoids you wasting time.
- Knowing which questions to ask from the start is key to only doing the required work at the right time and can ultimately save you working towards a dead end and wasted time/money.
- Working with advisers who have strong links to lenders who can save you money in fees.

The Importance of the Right Tax Advice

By Darren Clegg

A client of mine purchased a townhouse with the intention of placing it into trust for his young children. I was not involved in the purchase itself but subsequently was appointed as a trustee. Sometime after completing the purchase, I received a letter from a firm of accountants stating that having reviewed the Land Registry records relating to the sale and they were confident they could secure a substantial refund on the SDLT already paid for a fee of 30% of any saving made. The letter gave no further indication as to the basis upon which the claim for reimbursement was founded.

Wanting to secure the refund but unwilling to part with 30% of any monies recovered, I sought advice from another accountant who reviewed the transaction and advised that because the property had previously been designated for council tax as a house and separate self-contained basement flat, the purchase price could properly be divided between the two and Multiple Dwelling Relief claimed retrospectively. This meant that instead of paying SDLT on circa £4million for the entire property, it would now be paid on circa £3million for the house and circa £1million for the basement flat, taking a large portion of the price out of the SDLT top rate band. The overall effect of making this simple adjustment would be to reduce the SDLT payable on the purchase by £172,000.

This was done and the claim was accepted without challenge by HMRC and a cheque received for the overpayment. The fee paid to the accountant for his advice was £500. It was money well spent. My client was absolutely delighted with the savings made and the conveyancing solicitor who acted on the purchase was spared a negligence claim for failing in her duty of care to ensure all relevant SDLT reliefs are identified and applied at the time of the purchase.

HMRC and National Insurance Charge

By Ashley Smith

This was a family-owned company whose business was exploiting the writing skills of its two directors. The company owned a property, occupied by the two directors. The directors paid the bills relating to the property, but the taxpayer paid for structural repairs to the property. In order to remove the income tax charge an adjustment was put through the director's company loan accounts.

However, we ended up in the tax tribunal as HMRC were insistent that there should be a National Insurance charge, due to the delay between the original costs and compensating these by the adjustments in the accounts. The primary legislation requires a charge to income tax to exist in order for there to be a charge to National Insurance. Therefore, as expected the tribunal agreed with our argument that this should not arise.

HMRC frequently argue for a purposive approach to legislative interpretation when it suits their case, and in many instances, they are successful when such an approach is adopted by the courts and tax tribunals. The narrow approach they adopted in this case was therefore somewhat surprising and demonstrates an inconsistency in their approach to statutory interpretation. It would appear that they are not averse to adopting a narrow and more literal approach when the circumstances of the case suits them to do so.

Principal Private Residence Relief

By Ashley Smith

Make sure you qualify for principal private residence relief, don't just assume.

King Lear bought a property for £890,000 and lived in it. He then decided to demolish the original house and build his dream house, the demolishing and the rebuilding was a much more cost-effective strategy than renovation of the original property. The new house was built on new foundations out of different materials.

King Lear then had relationship and financial difficulties, so decided to sell the new house for £1,750,000. He assumed that the gain would be tax free, as he assumed that principal private residence (PPR) relief would apply.

Unfortunately HMRC disagreed.

The point that they relied on was that King Lear did not 'properly' live in the new house before he sold it. The demolition of the old house meant that the new house had to be considered separately. The houses were deemed to be different dwellings, so King Lear's occupation of the old house was irrelevant. King Lear's intention to live in the new house was not enough. He therefore failed to show a period of quality occupation in the new house, which would have led to it being treated as his home.

Unfortunately although PPR is generous it can be lost quite easily sometimes for illogical reasons; this is not always appreciated.

Inheritance Tax Nightmare

By Anonymous

Any mortgage advisor can pick a deal from a sourcing system and apply to a lender but that ignores the true value and essence of top-notch advice. The real merit and advantage comes from experience, knowledge and really getting under the skin of what a client is looking to do and why. Fully understanding circumstances and using those to the clients own advantage is exactly where it's at.

As an illustration, let's start with the story of two sisters – let's call them Emilia and Alice.

Both were still grieving the loss of their father whilst untangling the financials of his will. Dad had built up a small portfolio of high value properties. Upon his death he had wanted four of these investment properties to be left to the daughters. Emilia had only purchased her own house a few years earlier – Alice was still living at home with her mum and therefore was still a first-time buyer. Neither had official landlord experience.

The properties left by their late father were valued for probate purposes and they had a hefty inheritance tax bill to pay which came to over £975,000. Sadly, Dad had passed with no life insurance and in this case the properties had remaining mortgages secured against them in Dad's personal name.

By the time the two sisters approached us, they had been trying to find a mortgage advisor who could help for many years. No-one had come up with a solution that actually worked as yet. Most advisers were looking to push them into taking a bridging loan to pay off the existing debts, then to register the properties in their names before then selling the properties to a limited company SPV; a costly exercise. This plan was obviously being based upon combatting the harsh tax regime for personally geared landlords and the level of rental income that the properties generated.

Since their father had wanted the properties to be left to his daughters, as is often the case the advice came that the properties needed to be registered in the beneficiaries names first – but this was a 'Catch 22' as the property couldn't be registered to them without paying off the mortgages and the sizeable Inheritance Tax (IHT bill), a not uncommon situation. No-one so far had looked at the overall plan and the end goal, the prior insistence was a stepped process which was painful and costly – others were quoting finance based on what the clients thought they needed to get, which practically wasn't smooth or efficient.

Our adviser was able to draw up a plan that allowed the sisters to skip the step of registering the properties in their name first, instead would see them getting a mortgage to buy the properties directly from the estate into their newly set-up tax efficient SPV Limited Company. This was the best way to skip the step of registering the properties in their personal names.

As the sisters were beneficiaries of the estate, in tandem with their accountant's advice, we could look to create a Directors Loan Account (or DLA) to cover the deposit and fees from what would be the residue of the estate.

This removed the need for a bridging loan which would save circa £25,000 in fees straight away. As they had now been managing the properties for the estate, we were able to take the case to a prominent SPV lender with whom we have strong links. We could now show that they had some limited experience albeit not the experience that lenders would always ratify. This was without having had any buy to let property owned in their name which is so often the required benchmark to allow lending.

We managed to get the application agreed upfront and accepted and submitted it based on our initial detailed narrative making a strong argument to lend.

All was going well with underwriting until we obtained the valuation reports back – the properties had been down-valued heavily - by around £582,000 compared to the valuations that had been done for probate.

The case took a huge step backwards and left the sisters and us in the nightmare position of being unable to borrow the amount that was required to clear the estates liabilities. We had solved one seemingly insurmountable problem only to be faced with yet another.

However, we had an angle to work on, and whilst our adviser was looking for a way forward the resolution came.

The original valuations had been used to calculate the IHT liability. Those original valuations had been damned by the new RICS qualified surveyor during the remortgage process. Much of this shortfall was down to them having to pay that previously calculated tax liability – here we had a different professional surveyor who was stating that the properties were worth significantly less.

Our adviser contacted the solicitors to put the case forward for a lower IHT bill. The solicitors disagreed, and simply argued that the valuation they had done at the time of death needed to be used despite the new lower valuations. It was an extremely difficult situation for everyone but especially for the sisters. We were arguing over a huge sum in tax that they were being told they had to pay, but they now couldn't borrow enough money to clear this hefty tax bill and the current mortgages.

Would they have to sell the very properties that had been their late father's legacy?

Stalemate ensued for a long time, nothing would give – we knew it didn't seem fair but we are not solicitors or tax experts so it was difficult for us to get too entrenched in the situation.

Knowing our adviser" view on the subject and at our client's request, a conference call with all parties was arranged. Everyone listened as the solicitors explained all of their reasons as to why nothing could be done, the nightmare that we thought was well on the way to being solved was now in lockdown. What the solicitors were saying did not make any sense, they still had their calculations based on the properties being registered to the sisters first. The accountant was then making their calculations on the back of that.

To us, that step was not necessary – a Limited Company is a separate legal entity therefore they could buy the property directly from the estate. If they were buying the property directly from the estate, the estate would have to pay tax based on the proceeds of sale not based on the property value at time of death. We knew the properties were not worth anymore as we had done everything possible to get them valued at the initial amount without any success and therefore, if the IHT bill was less, the clients would have enough money to be able to complete the transaction and clear the real IHT bill.

The solicitor still disagreed, the accountant could only advise based on what the solicitor said and we still didn't appear to be getting anywhere, stalemate again ensued.

With everything remaining very protracted, we managed to get the solicitor to take a barrister's opinion, the first letter the solicitor wrote still did not cover all of the points that both the clients and we as broker were trying to argue, so we had to get them to go back again a second time.

On the second occasion there was a real breakthrough, the barrister was able to provide actual case law to show that what we wanted to do was in fact possible and there had been a precedent set. The clients managed to successfully challenge the IHT liability and save the incredible sum of £225,000.

The transaction progressed and to this day the two sisters continue to rent their properties to tenants. Their properties sit in a tax efficient SPV Ltd company for the foreseeable future. Nightmare solved.

Lessons learned:

- Never take no for an answer, until you know it's entirely justifiable.
- Have the best advisers around you that you can get, don't scrimp on fees if ultimately the quality of the advice can save you infinitely more than the cost of said fees.

Chapter 12

Insurance and Finance

The Tenant Who Set Himself On Fire

By Luke Behenna

It was pretty much a normal working day for me, the sun was shining and awake at 6:30am to get ready for the day. As I do every morning, I had a scroll through the news to see what events were happening, and I came across an article which caught my eye.

"Fire Brigade and Police called to property" the article described how a top floor flat in a terrace property had caught alight the previous evening. I thought nothing more about it at that point, I went about my daily routine and came in to work. As soon as the office was ready to open, we received a phone call from a customer. It is very rare for someone to call in at 9am on a Thursday morning, especially this particular client whom I very rarely heard from.

So with a friendly greeting I asked him how things were going and if business was good, to which he came back and said very bluntly, one of my properties caught fire last night, did you see the news? At this point I realised that a massive claim was about to be made. I asked them to come into the office and we could start the claims procedure. He turned up at around midday, we sat over a cup of coffee and started to collect information for the insurer. The details were horrific; it's a case I will never forget.

The client informed me that the tenant was on housing benefit, that was something we were well aware of having done a review the year prior of their various policies. It was apparent that the tenant in question, was an alcoholic and has been on a downward slope for some time and the Police received several calls from the tenant making threats to set themselves on fire and take out the property with it.

The events that followed when the Police arrived can only be described as very tragic and sad for the tenant who was in the position that they were in. Unfortunately, these were no threats, the customer informed me that the tenant in question poured petrol over themselves and lit a lighter, following that they jumped from a first storey window with the Police and paramedics below. To make the situation even worse, the tenants in the flat below were a young family. I can only imagine the fear it must have caused them as the situation unfolded. The firefighters arrived and extinguished the fire, so the first thing we had to do was assess the damage. It could only be described as the very charred remains of where someone used to live. There was damage from where the firefighters had used their hoses to extinguish the fire, so the first thing we had to do was get the insurer to approve the use of industrial dehumidifiers and extractors to dry the property out, this took around three weeks day and night to fully dry the property.

Having sent pictures to the insurers, they then approved works to commence to get the property ripped out and repaired. The overall cost of the repairs ended up being over £47,000 net of the customer's excess of £250. It was very lucky that we had reviewed the customer's insurance policy the year prior and had we not confirmed that the tenant was indeed on housing benefit, it would have resulted in the customer being without cover and the claim being declined.

Top tip:

Be honest with your insurer, as little white lies can become great black clouds that can be very costly.

The Storm And The Solar Panel

By Luke Behenna

The UK sometimes experiences extreme weather and inevitably there are bound to be a few claims arising for broken fences and flying roof slates. I had a call one early morning from a customer. The customer called to inform us that the neighbouring property had lost one of its solar panels and it had dropped several metres and landed on the customer's asbestos roof.

Within an hour of finishing the call, I was at the premises to assess the damage. The solar panel had not only knocked through the roof but had slid down the steep pitch of the roof and was now wedged and hanging off between the two buildings. The important point in this story is that the property's roof was around 15 metres high so it was not a simple job of getting a ladder up and patching the roof over.

Once the information had been supplied to the insurer, they started to question the weather conditions and if this was indeed due to storm damages. This is where I, as a broker, needed to support our client in making a legitimate claim. We scoured through the weather reports for the area and submitted the information to the insurer which confirmed the high and gusty winds along with the weather pattern for the three days prior to confirm this.

Once the insurer gave us the approval that we had a valid claim, that's when the hard work began. We had to find contractors who would work with asbestos, who as you can imagine, are quite limited in number. Weeks had gone by and we had to contact various national and local contractors to quote for the job. We must have gone through about 7-8 different contractors who all refused to do the job. Eventually we found the one golden egg who said they were happy to price and worked with asbestos on various commercial and residential premises. Great, the hard bit was done, all we needed now was someone to put up the internal and external scaffolding and we were good to go. Within another week we had all the quotes we needed to submit to the insurer for their approval.

The green light was given five days later (after a few nudges) to get the works completed. The contractor did his bit and things were sorted.

Top tip:

- Again, the point we need to take away from this, is that the roof was asbestos, so many insurers will not cover asbestos for the exact same reasons we had during the claim. It's very costly and time consuming, again be honest with your insurance company, it will earn you many brownie points in the long run.

The Lightning Bolt And The Chimney Stack

By Luke Behenna

We are back with a storm claim, this one was meant to be a very straightforward claim, but the insurance company made it far more difficult than it needed to be. The customer owned a property which had a flat let on the second floor, a pretty standard setup and nicely furnished. The weather the night before was awful, it was like something out of a film, lightning blowing up the sky, quite majestic and beautiful but very powerful when hitting bricks and mortar.

My client rang me late one evening. They had received a call from their tenant confirming that they had heard a loud bang and crash in the loft. They assumed some slates had come off and smashed and based on this assumption I asked the client to call me when they were at the site. When they got there, they called to say it was much more serious and this had me prepared for the worst. The lightning had struck the chimney stack and blown a hole through the gable, with bits of the gable smashing through the insulation and into the kitchen.

To give you some idea of how big the hole was, the customer was able to climb through the hole from the stairway through into the loft. Having submitted all the information to the insurer as per normal procedure, the insurer came back very quickly and declined to honour the claim. The first thing that ran through my mind was, why decline? How can this be a decline, it's a straightforward storm damage claim? After trying to contact the person dealing with the claim and having no success, I called the insurers claims number and luckily got through to the claims manager for property and liability.

Having explained the whole situation to the claims manager and having explained how the previous handler must have misread the policy wording and wrongly declined, the customers claim was then honoured and a settlement of £5,200 was given, plus a good will gesture was added to the claim. What I learnt from a broker perspective is to always look for insurers who don't use call centres to handle claims. This is now something we factor in before we consider working with an insurer.

Top tip:

- Get your broker to read the policy wording as when the insurer tries to decline a claim, the expert needs to work on your behalf and show them that they are wrong.

£120,000 Entrance Fee!

By Roy Inman

I had lost £120,000, nearly destroyed the relationship with a close friend and been diagnosed with depression. It had been the most expensive lesson and entrance fee ever.

Just before the recession, I had grown my portfolio aggressively and at the same time I'd got so fed up with agents not managing my properties properly that I'd also brought all the management in house and I was dealing with this myself. I had been fulltime in property for over a year leaving my catering career behind. The biggest challenge I'd faced was adjusting to the speed of the real world instead of the speed of working in a kitchen where your next deadline was only a few hours away at the next mealtime and the pace of service was on another level. In the real world everything took days and weeks to do what I deemed to be the simplest of things, and I was used to working in minutes and hours. I had never worked in a corporate environment or had any experience in managing that environment and this became an expensive lesson.

I had two main skills, one in the kitchen as a chef, cooking and managing high-speed, high-level kitchen and two, sourcing and structuring property deals. I had my power team to do this but was lacking in the property management team. I'd had so many bad experiences with agents that I gave up trying and just thought 'I could do a better job myself'. So I took over all the management of my properties whilst still continuing to buy.

At the time there was a lot less work to do with property management than there is today, there was a lot less regulation, paperwork and time involvement required in general. However it was something that you still needed to enjoy doing, and, although yes, I could do a better job than the agents, I soon came to realise that I didn't actually enjoy doing it all that much. In hindsight, would I go the same way again? Probably not! A good managing agent is worth their weight in gold and will look after, manage, and protect your assets, freeing you up to focus on what you want to do, whether that is to grow your portfolio, spend time with your family, or follow your dreams and hobbies.

As I mentioned earlier, I was still buying and building my portfolio which I loved doing and as with all human nature you spend time doing the things you enjoy and avoid/procrastinate on the things you don't (even when they need to and should be done).

I was brought up with strong values around money and the way you treat people. I'd always paid off every penny of my debts and paid every bill on time. I always aimed to treat people the way I expected to be treated and believed others would do the same. I grew up in Swanage, a small town on the South Coast, with a population of less than 10,000 people. It's a beautiful seaside town that is perfect for bringing up children. There is, however, one conflicting positive/negative with it and that is that you are sheltered from the real world or at least a different world. I ended up having to learn the hard way that people don't always have the same values as you do.

In my mind, I thought and truly believed that people would pay their bills, including their rent, as a priority just like I did. At the time it was all I knew and believed so I focused on doing the things I enjoyed doing and avoided the things that I didn't. I did not realise that this was the calm before a storm that was building up behind me.

The account started to get short on money so I asked the solicitor to transfer £10,000 back from our general file where I had around £150,000 on account for purchases, and then a few weeks later another £10,000 to top the accounts up. I was so busy speaking to vendors and agents, solicitors, brokers and pulling deals together that I didn't think too much of it and thought it would all be okay once I got the next few deals sorted.

By this time we were now in the thick of the recession and things started to get bad and I mean really bad. Before I knew it, I was losing nearly £20,000 a month, yes £20,000 a month! That was when it really hit home that there was a problem, things were such a mess.

I didn't know where to start. Do I focus on doing more deals to bring the money in? Do I chase people for rent? Do I apply to the courts for eviction? Do I get quotes for the refurbs that need doing? I was overwhelmed with everything and my mind, judgement and thinking was clouded by the fact that I was losing £20,000 a month and things were going downhill fast.

Somehow, I decided I was going to stop buying and focus on sorting out the problem that was in front of me, and as I'm writing this, you'd think that would have just been the simple obvious answer. However, when you're in the thick of it for months with all the stress, hustle and busyness going on around you, facing the one thing that you instinctively avoid doing, it is a real struggle to get motivated. I now know that this is what happens to so many people once they hit overwhelm. I had no energy and had gone from leaping out of bed in the morning at 6am to dragging myself out at noon.

I'd seen the Doctor and been tested for pretty much everything including diabetes, and all sorts. They came up with nothing, they said there was nothing wrong with me. I knew there was something wrong, my wife knew there was something wrong, but we didn't know what and the Doctor gave me the all clear as if I was wasting their time. Things continued to build up and up, still losing close to £20,000 a month. Two months later, you would have seen me in the corner of my office room, curled up in a ball, just staring at a blank spot on the wall wondering what the hell I was going to do, and in that moment, I decided to go back to the Doctors.

Fortunately this time I saw a different Doctor, he went through everything with me again, checked my blood pressure, normal, checked all the test results, normal, asked me a few questions and then went quiet for what seemed like an eternity. I will never forget the next words that came out of his mouth. "Mr Inman, I don't think you are going to like what I am about to say to you but I'm going to say it anyway, you're suffering from depression. To help you get out of this cycle that you are in and to help you with your motivation and give you more energy I'm going to prescribe some mild antidepressants, they're not addictive and will be just enough to help you to get out of the vicious spiral that you are in. I would also recommend regular exercise as this will boost your endorphin levels and help to give you more energy and feel better". My head nearly exploded, all the thoughts you could possibly think of were going around in my head. 'There was no way whatsoever that I could possibly be depressed', 'I don't get depressed', and a few others I don't wish to repeat.

As I was leaving the Doctor's surgery holding my prescription, I started to think about why I was there, why I'd even come back to the Doctors after being told there was nothing wrong with me. I'd gone because I wanted to find an answer, I wanted to sort this mess out, I wanted things to change, I needed things to change. I had a responsibility to provide for myself, my wife and I owed my close friend £120,000 that I'd borrowed and most importantly my wife was pregnant with our first baby who was due in only a couple of months.

Was this the answer I'd been looking for, even if it wasn't the answer I wanted to hear? I didn't have any other answers, ideas or suggestions, so I decided to trust the Doctor and go with it as I had no other options and had to do something and so I headed for the pharmacy, collected my tablets and took the first one before I changed my mind.

I headed home and told my wife, whom I can never thank enough for supporting me through everything she has over the 13 years we have been together, and who may never really understand how truly grateful I am.

I now had a plan. I also started to do exercise to help get my body going and boost my endorphins. I also jumped on Amazon and bought a book about overcoming depression. I was all in now and looking to get over this and move forward. The book arrived within a week of me going to see the Doctor and I started to read it. By the time I had finished chapter two I had made the decision right there and then that this wasn't me. I wasn't accepting this and that I needed to step up and sort my life out. I wasn't going to be a husband struggling with depression. I wanted to be the best kind of father to our child.

I continued to take the tablets for a few more days along with some exercise and whether it truly helped or just acted as a placebo I'll never know. What I do know is that I felt better and was getting on very well with the workload and problems that I'd allowed to build up. Don't get me wrong there was a long way to go, I was still losing over £10,000 a month and I had just come to the real understanding of how long things take when you bring courts into the equation when having to evict tenants along with the cost of court and bailiff fees. I was on the right track but it was going to take months to sort and if I didn't get it sorted soon there was a very high chance that I would end up defaulting on mortgages and lose everything. On top of that, I had one last thing I needed to do. I needed to tell my close friend that I'd lost over £100,000 and that I couldn't repay the remaining £20,000 as I needed it to help me while I tried to turn things around.

As you can probably imagine this conversation didn't go well, as they had re-mortgaged their house to lend me this money on the proviso that I would always have it to pay back. They were very angry and very stressed about it all and responded like any normal person would in that situation. Things were said that would only ever be said in that extremely stressed situation and this put a huge strain on our relationship for many years. At the time they couldn't see how I could possibly ever repay that amount of money and things were very difficult between us for a long time. I had been brought up to always pay my debts and pay my debts I would, somehow!

Over the following six months, with my back firmly against the wall, I battled through the mountain of paperwork spread around my office, made applications to courts to evict non-paying tenants, oversaw refurbishment works, called in favours from friends to help with some refurb projects to keep costs down, re-let the properties and watched the near £20,000 a month loss move slowly to break even, through to being back in the black and then on to a very nice healthy cash flow. I'd turned everything around and it now just needed great on-going management and time to build back up and slowly over a few years I did just that.

This was by far one of the most stressful 18 months of my life but also where I gained so much experience and knowledge around managing property and tenants, especially through a recession and tough times. This is also why we are now an extremely strong business that is completely setup for any challenges that are thrown at us and have a very, very specific system that is very much operated from the principle of a 'Firm but Fair' basis. At the time I could have lost everything, a multi-million-pound property portfolio, the income that provided for us, my relationship with my close friend, my confidence, my pride and who knows what else.

This alone is why it's such a great reason to have a good letting agency who can manage your portfolio for you, whether it's 1 or 100 properties. It takes all the stress and worry away and ensures that everything is kept up to date, fully compliant, your properties well looked after with your tenants paying their rent so that you can spend your time doing the things you love and enjoy.

All the experience and knowledge in not only property management, but investing has come from the sometimes very difficult times, as well as when things are going well. If you meet anyone who says that everything's easy and that it will be a walk in the park, in my opinion and the opinion of many other investors and business owners that I have had the privilege of calling friends over the years, they are either liars or they haven't really done that much or been in business that long. If it was easy, everyone would be doing it.

The truth is that nothing is ever easy all of the time, there are always challenging times and it is getting through those challenging times and how you deal with them that moulds and defines you. It's how you step up to the responsibility that is put before you and deal with it. When you have responsibility for something and you look at the true meaning of the word, broken down and really understood it you have the ability to respond, now how you choose to respond is your choice but you have been given that ability and the outcome and future is yours to make as you will.

Early Repayment Charge Nightmare

By Anonymous

One of the toughest elements of the job, is dealing with third parties, either a business or individual that we have no control over but are absolutely essential to getting the job done. Because we deal with a great many surveyors, solicitors, accountants, lenders and estate agents, a good broker should hold them accountable and question their advice or actions where we feel things can be done better, but at the same time collaborating with everyone in the process to tie the ends together. I am sure any good third party should also hold brokers accountable for their advice too!

Of course, we always tread carefully and diplomatically because it's not our domain, but it doesn't mean that we don't learn a huge amount about other parties' responsibilities that then allow us to question other professions and get them to justify their decisions!

One such example is as follows.

Here's the back story. Before he contacted us, our future client was looking to buy a new home to live in. He called the lender for his current home, and they explained that he could port his current mortgage to his new home to avoid him paying the hefty early repayment charges which existed, in other words, move the mortgage from his current residence across to his new home. He found a great property with real potential but it needed some heavy refurbishment work which meant he couldn't move his current mortgage straight away, instead he used bridging finance to acquire this new home.

Following the refurb, that was done to a very high standard, he was then ready to move his mortgage over, he was then told by the lender that you cannot 'port' a mortgage onto a property you already own, they were suggesting that he would have to pay the hefty penalty he had been trying to avoid doing from the beginning.

Ouch. This left our client facing tough Early Repayment Charges in excess of 20,000 Whole English Pounds and on the strangest of annoying technicalities.

He was an existing customer of the lender, but none of that mattered as his mortgage advisor there told him in no uncertain terms that nothing could be done, full stop. No further help, assistance or a way forward offered.

At this point the gentleman approached us. Exactly the type of client that should be taken seriously but are all too often taken for granted by huge global corporate banks. We could have realistically brokered a deal to any lender to obtain a mortgage for him, this would have been the easy route, but at the same time, one that would cost over £23,000, not something we could gloss over or ignore, a serious amount of money for anyone to lose over a basic nonsensical technicality.

Not prepared to allow this to happen, our adviser took this exact same case and exact same scenario back to the lender.

As is paramount in these situations, we 'put pen to paper' so to speak, aggrieved that this hadn't been sorted out by the lender, but at the same time, a chance to prove ourselves and win this client's trust for life.

We presented all of the facts and the existing relationships fully, gave full context to the case and put our weight behind the basic fact that this client had been in no doubt that this couldn't move any further, but queried why the lender felt that this was in any way treating this client fairly. We gave a full breakdown of what had happened and what the client's future plans were. After serious consideration, the lender felt that they had been at fault and were now prepared to make the exception to their misplaced 'company policy' - a huge result.

Yes, the lender had to go to serious effort to create a workaround on their systems, but our interjection had managed to get our client the mortgage he was told he couldn't have.

The advice on the original mortgage product was no different to what he had received originally but with the execution of this application in our hands, the response was completely different and we achieved the desired result.

It would have been much quicker and easier for us to take him to another lender, at one point, our client even wanted to give up and try another lender, paying the £23,000 penalty as he thought our efforts were likely to be futile, but ultimately, they weren't. We not only saved our now client this significant sum, but we earned in the process, and created a huge amount of goodwill resulting in fantastic referrals and future business. And the lender retained their client!

Chapter 13

Fire Safety

Fire Safety – An Introduction

By Sue Pope

The most important thing to remember about Fire Safety is that it is in place to protect lives.

Therefore, please bear in mind that it is not just all about what is "a legal requirement" there is also a moral obligation that must also be considered when making any decisions. Doing the bare minimum, or even doing less, hoping to get away with it, cutting corners, using cheap or substandard materials, etc. could mean that in the future, someone is very badly injured or even dies if there is a fire in your property. Please always do the right thing and consider all aspects before making your decisions. Below are three stories that I would like to share.

A True Story with Warnings

A lovely four storey property was being used as a holiday let. The new owner decided they didn't like or understand the information and advice they had been given by their holiday letting agent and didn't want to employ a Fire Risk Assessor so they contacted the Fire and Rescue Service and insisted they visit to give free help and advice.

They visited and gave very detailed and prescriptive advice in writing. The owners didn't like this advice, thought it was completely over the top and so contacted me for help. They didn't listen to any of my advice either but decided to listen to their electrician instead because they liked what he was telling them and this was far easier and cheaper to do. Needless to say, I walked away as I didn't want to continue my involvement, and sadly don't know the eventual outcome, but I do know it is not a holiday let, and therefore not producing any income anymore, and that once you are on the radar of an enforcing authority, they don't forget about you!

Top tips:

- If you invite the Fire and Rescue Service to visit and give advice, you need to follow it or face the consequences. The advice will usually be to the letter of the law (they can't do anything differently) and it will be prescriptive.
- Don't just follow the advice you like the sound of or is the cheapest option, it may not be the best option and then probably won't be compliant.

A Tenant with No Fire Extinguishers

By Sue Pope

I know of a sad story of a pub and flats above where they didn't have any fire extinguishers and experienced a fire. The untrained staff used a hosepipe to try to put it out, which then caused it to explode into a massive fire. The Fire and Rescue Service had to be called and there was serious damage to the property.

I was asked to assist by the landlord and acted as a link between the tenant, landlord and the Fire and Rescue Service. The aftermath of a fire can be a very stressful time, and unless you've been there before, you probably won't know what to do.

The Fire and Rescue Service will often serve an Enforcement or Prohibition notice on the property or parts thereof, and that notice must be taken seriously. It is a legal document and you must abide by its requirements. It may prevent the use of all or just part of the property, it may determine what remedial works have to be completed and to what standard before the notice can be lifted, and they will want to see proof of this during the works (just like Building Control). I would always advise you to take photos at key stages and these can also be included in the Fire Risk Assessment that will also be needed at the end.

The remedial works were extensive because of the amount of damage caused. As the Fire and Rescue Service had attended the fire, they automatically carry out a Fire Safety Audit, which looks into the details of the property, including the Construction, Fire Prevention and Protection Measures and how fire safety is managed throughout the property, by the various "Responsible Persons" (these are the people who have control over all or parts of the building, in this instance both the tenant and the landlord).

It was obviously very necessary in this case to educate the tenant and make sure that they did everything properly from then on. As the tenant was served with a Prohibition Notice, they could not reopen the pub, and was having trouble paying their rent. The landlord suffered financial loss on two counts, loss of rent and the cost of the remedial works, which they were unable to claim back from the tenant.

Top tips:

- Make sure your business tenants have an up-to-date Fire Risk Assessment (you should request a copy and share a copy of your FRA with them too).
- Make sure they have acted upon any findings in the FRA.
- Make sure they have the appropriate Fire Safety Equipment in place, and it is serviced/maintained as required.
- Make sure they have appropriate business insurance in place.
- Make sure all these points are requirements and are covered in the Lease.

HMO Disaster

By Sue Pope

On one occasion, I was asked to carry out a Fire Risk Assessment at an HMO property and found there were loads of problems. Some of the front doors weren't fire doors, others were poorly fitted fire doors, there was a lack of any suitable fire detection in the communal areas, incomplete fire detection in the flats, no emergency lighting, out of date fire extinguishers (and not enough of them), and an external fire escape (originally metal, but now mostly rust) that was a death trap.

I drew up a specification for all the things that needed to be rectified and sent it to the client, who's only response was that they couldn't believe it was that bad, and did it all really need to be done now, couldn't they just do some of it? The answer to that question was obviously no!

Some months later, I was asked by an estate agent to go back to see what had been done and sign off the FRA. It was even more of a disaster. They had supposedly done some of the work, but nothing had been done properly, some of the wiring appeared to be dangerous, the fire detection was a total mess and the external fire escape in a worse state than before. My new list was even longer, and to make it compliant, it was going to be very expensive.

Not long after, I was asked to visit the property again, but this time to meet the new owner, who had managed to buy the property for a really good price as so much work was needed. We worked on the project together with some good trades and after some "major surgery" especially to the electrics and fire detection they ended up with a good, and more importantly, compliant HMO.

Top tips:

- Get good advice from competent people.
- Follow the good advice. Ask questions and learn, so you'll know more for next time.
- Employ good tradespeople and use good quality materials.
- Work to the specifications and don't cut corners or do something different, check first.
- Keep checking everything is being done properly and to the required standards.
- Get your competent advisors to check during the work to ensure everything is being done properly.
- Make sure you get all the relevant Certification when the works are completed.

Chapter 14

Business Stories

The Best Deal Never Done

By Jackie Tomes

The property nightmare that never was. We'll call this the best deal that I ever didn't do.

It was a commercial conversion to 17 residential units (including adding additional storey to building). Total project cost was £2,018,861, and the Gross Development Value was £2,815,000.

Why did I think I was ready to take on this project? Well I had:

- Heard talks on doing developments and doing conversions,
- Attended courses on doing developments and doing conversions,
- Heard that "Doing a development is not much harder than a refurb (and we'd done lots of refurbs!) just bigger numbers"

I was ready to stop "wasting" time on the little refurb projects and to do some proper investing. I was ready to make millions in the shortest possible timeframe! I was fired up! Inspired! Ready to go big!

But this deal never happened. Luckily my mentor saved me from myself, by asking me questions that made me realise that there was still so much that I didn't know and didn't have lined up and that I was completely blind to the risks. If I were to forge on and do this with the 'go hard or go home' attitude, I'd be putting the multi-million-pound portfolio that I'd built over the last few years on the line.

No-one else in the property world was giving me this reality check. Moving into developments had started to seem straightforward from what I'd heard, and I'd got drawn into it.

Shortly after this stern talking to, I abandoned the project. I decided I wanted a stepping-stone out of doing single lets and refurbs, not a 'jump-out-of-a-plane-with-a-parachute-full-of-holes' situation!

It took over a year to find the right 'stepping-stone' into a commercial conversions project, but once I found it, it was ideal.

It was an empty shop on the ground floor, with three floors of residential above, on the outskirts of town. The three floors of residential were arranged as two-flats and had been in existence for many years. The plan was to convert the shop into two 1-bedroom flats and refurbish and regularise the two units already in existence above. Two flats and a shop converted into four flats. Simple!

This really was ideal as a first conversion for several reasons:

- All the conversion works were under Permitted Development which really helped to reduce any planning risk.
- The project was eligible for a £25,000 per unit interest free loan from the local authority to bring the empty units back into use, so £100k interest free loan for up to three years massively reduced the finance costs.
- Two units were already in existence meaning half of it was already residential, so in many ways only a 50% conversion and 50% heavy refurbishment!
- As it was a commercial property, there was no 3% stamp duty surcharge for second-home owners, helping to reduce upfront costs even further.

Nightmare on Sourcing Street!

By Tina Walsh

Being passionate about raising standards in the Property Sourcing Sector, I have worked with several investors over the past years assisting them to put together case files for appeals to Redress Schemes; in an attempt to regain cash paid out for very poor service and in some instances simply disgraceful behaviour!

I could give several examples of poor sourcing services but I suppose one stands out more than others.

An inexperienced investor contacted a sourcing agent and was looking to buy a simple two or three bedroom buy to let property, a first step in what was hoped would be a long-term relationship with property investment and the building up of a property portfolio for cash flow.

The criteria for the property to be purchased were fairly simple really, two or three bedroom terraced property, good rental area, would consider currently tenanted properties, light refurbishment (redecoration and cleaning) only, no major work such as structural or major interior work. The investor had limited funds for any refurbishment work following purchase.

Several conversations took place and eventually details of a property were sent over to the investor for their consideration.

The property details provided were for a two-bedroom terraced property described as currently tenanted with a long-term tenant who was very happy to stay. Currently in good condition, with only minor repairs required but not urgent as the tenant was quite happy.

The sourcing fee was £1,500 and the agent would manage the property for the investor after the purchase was complete.

The investor arranged to view the property with the sourcing agent. At the viewing, the sourcer rushed them through the property, not allowing time to take a careful look at condition or chat with the current tenant. They asked for another viewing but their request was sidelined, ignored or the subject changed, but following reassurances from the sourcing agent, who had come highly recommended, and under some pressure to pay a holding deposit, the investor secured the property and proceeded to purchase.

Once purchased a lot of issues came to light following a visit to the property and a chat with the existing tenant:

- The local authority had issued an enforcement order for certain works to be completed on the property due to its poor condition (the sourcer later admitted that they had been aware but failed to inform the investor).
- The tenant had made several complaints about a lot of serious issues that had been ignored and was far from happy (the sourcer admitted that they had been aware but again, failed to inform the investor).
- The condition of the property was far from 'Good'.
- A flat roof extension had serious leak issues and needed completely replacing.

Following on from the local authority report, a survey was arranged and paid for by the investor. The survey report outlined many serious issues with the property and it was estimated that initial costs for the repairs would be in the region of £20,000; not the 'light' redecoration and clean that had been asked for.

The investor asked the sourcing agent to refund the sourcing fee paid and compensate them for the high level of repair work that had been required, that they had known about but not disclosed; they refused. The investor approached me and asked for my help. Together we pulled together a file of evidence and submitted a formal complaint letter to the sourcing agent, who at that time was a member of a Redress Scheme but not registered for either Data Protection Supervision or AML Supervision.

The letter of complaint was initially ignored but there then followed months of exchanges of emails and on several different occasions financial compensation was agreed only to fail at the point at which payment should have been made. The financial and mental stress that the whole situation invoked was immense causing long-term physical illness for the investor.

So much stress was caused that the investor did not pursue the complaint and sold the property just to get rid of the problem, despite a large loss of cash. I know that those of you who are experienced investors will say that a lot more checks should have been carried out such as another viewing insisted upon, a survey carried out prior to purchase, but hindsight is a wonderful thing and we were all ‘new investors’ at the start of our own journeys.

The lesson might be to not take at face value recommendations from anyone, and understand property investing yourself first, before you trust the word of anyone; including a sourcing agent.

As a caveat to this case, I would say that there is a place in the property investment sector for sourcing agents, but only those who operate professionally, honestly and within the letter of the law; at the end of the day it might well still be ‘buyer beware’ as the emotional cost of seeking financial recompense can be high!

Introduction To The World Of Locksmiths

By Dean Girvin

When the majority of us close our front doors, lift the handles, and turn the key, we assume our homes are secure and safe from intrusion. We keep a large percentage of our most treasured possessions behind a locked door, such as jewellery, electronics, photographs to name a few, but how many of us can say we've been to a store to buy high quality locks for doors or even ask a local expert locksmith for security advice on locking products to help keep our homes and businesses protected?

Locksmithing is a profession that can technically be traced back to around 4,000 years ago in Ancient Egypt and locks were originally made from wood. The developments and advancement in locks took around another thousand years with the introduction of metal locks and this development can be credited to the Ancient Romans. As in all trades and crafts, huge steps forwards and engineering continue to enhance the development of all types of locks, many of which can still he found working to this present day.

The Smell

One of my most memorable and unforgettable jobs that I have ever been involved with came about through a letting agency that had been using my services for many years. The landlord had fallen out with the tenant over a number of issues such as monies owed and gaining access to the property for boiler servicing and inspections.

A date for the tenant moving out had been set with plenty of notice given to both parties. On the given time and date I had arrived about 15 minutes earlier, had a quick check of the locks involved and then waited for the landlord and letting agents. The agreed time of noon had arrived. It was a very warm and sunny day and I proceeded to gain access with the tools as the original keys the letting agents held did not work as the tenant had changed locks.

After a short period the lock was picked and door opened. I was immediately hit with an overwhelming foul stench and nose burning smell; a smell you could taste. We were very reluctant to enter the building to investigate the source of the smell, it quickly became obvious the source was the bathroom. The source of the stench was in the bath. The tenant had been using the bath as the toilet for what I guessed was about four to five weeks. Good luck finding someone to clean that lot out, I thought to myself.

Surprise Eviction

Tenant evictions sometimes do not always involve picking or bypassing locks. One of my easiest jobs was an invitation from a landlord booking myself and the bailiff, at a predetermined date and time, to repossess the property following the long process of an eviction.

We assembled outside the garden gate anticipating what awaited us. At the given time, the bailiff proceeded to announce himself and that we were going to enter. I had already seen a tricky lock on the front door and started processing my options. No answer to the bailiff's announcement, and he then asked me to gain entry. I said I was just going to pop around the back, to see what doors and locks were there.

Through the garden gate I went around to the rear garden and what did I find? The sliding patio door was open. The rear back door was open and all the rear windows were open. Happy days, I thought. I then proceeded to call everyone round and in we went. At the rear of the property the decking that had been installed by the landlord a couple years ago prior, was completely stripped and gone. Inside the property, the boiler was disconnected and gone, radiators in every room were taken, the kitchen cupboard doors had gone, and for some bizarre reason they had taken down a bedroom ceiling. All very costly repairs for the unfortunate landlord.

Devious Ex Partners

One evening I got a call to a local housing estate as a young man had locked himself and his brother out of a property. I arrived and they seemed very genuine and eager to get back inside the home. I asked for ID as normal, but he told me everything inside the house was not a problem once you let us in. The lock was picked in about 15 minutes and I let them go in. "How much do I owe you?" they asked as I was putting my tools away. I let him know that I needed some form of ID.

He proceeded to go from room to room opening drawers and cupboards, but after 10 minutes still nothing. I was getting very suspicious and annoyed as he could not even produce a photograph of himself in the property.

The excuses flowed and he kept trying to get me to leave. I explained I was calling the Police, which I did. The Police turned up and I explained the situation and he confessed to them this was his ex-partners house. She was away in the services and he had moved out about three months ago and wanted to get back in to get the rest of his belongings. I let the Police do their jobs and just reminded myself you get to meet all sorts of people in this line of work.

Common Mistakes Investors Make

By Vicki Wusche

Lesson One – Passion vs. Experience

I realised I have always been passionate about property; I just did not have the language and framework to understand it before my first training course. Literally within days of my first property training event ending, my family group and I had picked our area and planned our first trip. Within weeks we had two offers accepted and I hadn't even taken my second property class yet.

We were overconfident, especially after just two hours of training, determined and carried away with my passion and purpose. The first offer that was accepted was on a beautiful Victorian three bed terrace; it was half double glazed with a dated bathroom and a light refurb needed. Our offer of £74,000 on £98,000 asking price was accepted and we were off.

Then came the lessons:

I was excited to receive our first survey report so I read every detail and was shocked to see a retention because "chimney breasts had been removed without proper structural support" and "subsidence"! Our response involved an emergency drive from London to Liverpool to re-inspect the property and check the comments in the survey, as our photos did not specifically or sufficiently show us the rooms in question.

In our case it was the surveyor's "cut and paste" mistake that nearly cost us the mortgage and the deal.

The chimney breasts were exactly where they should be, but the previous owner had removed the stone hearth and so there was a gap in the carpet. There simply was no subsidence as it was a mid-terrace property and was firmly held in place.

My next property venture went on to teach me about plaster cracks and subsidence, rising damp, leaking gutters and condensation mould and that was just a few of the lessons to be learnt! I am so passionate about this bit of property investing – the classic property faults that can save you wasted time and expenses that I created a workshop, I could share my experience with my mentees. Make a plan about how you will accelerate this part of your knowledge.

Key points:

- Understand property as a structure – I bought time with a surveyor to learn about property and surveys, cracks and mould.
- Take better photos at the first viewing – create a system for your property inspection/viewings and always follow it.
- Be careful when challenging a surveyor even if you are right – a surveyor's professionalism, insurance cover and therefore business, are all tightly linked. Even when you are right, carefully plan how you complain to get the outcome you want and remember everything in a straightforward mortgage valuation is deniable!

Lesson Two - Understand your market

This might seem obvious, but I meet so many new investors who are just focusing on the geographic area and the maths of a deal. These are important, but your market is not just about which streets to buy in and which to avoid, and not just the maths of individual deals. You need to really understand the people of the area, your prospective market, and your clients. What do they like and what do they loathe?

Back in early 2008, we were so "London" that we stuck out in Liverpool like an alien landing in the village pub! Luckily a local letting agent took us by the scruff of the neck and shook sense into us, sadly not before we had wasted over £500 in unnecessary work, not to mention time.

Know the style and preference of the tenant market you are aiming for. Give them more than they expect, but still within their taste spectrum. Focus on the details like laminate vs. carpets, blinds vs. curtains, feature walls vs. magnolia throughout.

One of our biggest challenges was where the bathroom was going to be placed. So many Victorian properties have downstairs bathrooms that were added to the back of the kitchen. You need to understand the competition and whether relocating a bathroom is essential or more about your preferences. Your task is simply to make the prospective tenant fall in love with the property.

Key points:

- Every area will be different; your goal is to make your property fly out the letting agents door.
- It takes local knowledge – don't be afraid to ask for advice from the very people whose job it will be to let your property.

Lesson Three - No emotion only maths

You can see the tell-tale signs of over excitement and "emotion", all the way through the detail of my first deal. Pride, passion and sheer-will dominated over common sense, clear planning and understanding the financials.

It was only natural given our inexperience and it was compounded by the fact that we were a family group on this first deal. All working together, refurbishing the house together, each with our own ideas. Quick lesson here – decide on a leader or manager and then, only the manager makes the decisions. As those of you who know me or know of me can imagine, the next 100 houses were led by me.

We had been to a few more property training sessions by the time the deal completed and we had to start working on the refurbishment. Bob, my partner, is an electrician by profession and our brother-in-law is both an architect and a plumber, but that did not mean we were any better at making finance focused decisions – that is a different skill.

There are three key money points:

1. The first is based on the financial mechanism you are using to buy the investment. Understanding all the costs up front, especially the impact of interest and fees is crucial. Build your investment model on Net Return on Investment (ROI) as this is a truer reflection of a deal's profitability.

    a. Create two sets of numbers – straight forward profit based on costs and then profit based on contingencies – here you add an allowance for repairs and three-year maintenance. Often investors use 10-20% allowance, but this depends on level of initial refurb, and of course the tenants and securities you put in place.

    b. Then comes the deal itself. Does it work for you and for the buyer? I know there is social media pressure to get the best deal, drive the hardest bargain, but I want to leave the seller able to move on.

    c. In the period 2008-2010 there were a lot of repossessions and people were struggling. Reducing the price by £4,000 would save me £1,000 cash and cost me the interest charge on £3,000 of increased mortgage cost, but that £4,000 could make all the difference to the seller. That small change in offer price had a marginal impact on my ROI figures.

    d. I want a deal if it hits my target ROI. I always offer lower than I need, in order to get a refusal first. Then I always get my second offer accepted. I don't want to lose a deal that meets my criteria because of greed. My strategy is long-term and properly calculated.

2. My second measure is to know that six months occupancy and full rent will cover 12 months mortgage payments and 20% light refurb budget. That is how I mitigate my risk, so

check the maths on the monthly profit as well as the ROI to be sure.

a. Once the deal is complete then it's all about how you prepare the property to rent or re-sell. They are two different markets with two different mathematical models.

b. I always focus on Buy to Let. My pre-offer calculations included a budget and 15% contingency to cover the refurbishment costs and therefore second and subsequent years would generate even more profit. My goal is to be the best house to let on the street. I want my properties filled by referral.

c. You can see there is no place for emotion, only the maths and a sprinkle of humanity. Needless to say, that is not how this deal went.

3. I think I understood something was wrong before I received the mortgage offer, and quickly realised we were heading for 2008 style mortgage fraud with a "morning purchase" at one price followed by "afternoon resale" at 100% valuation to create a "No Money Down Deal."

a. Luckily for us, The Council of Mortgage lenders brought in the "6-month rule" you all know and love, so we had to get a new last-minute lender and second offer.

b. If you are working with mentors or sourcers that put you in touch with their brokers - make sure you understand the debt you are committing to and that you are totally happy with the risks and contracts.

c. There is no return from mortgage fraud, we had a very narrow escape!

We then overspent on the refurbishment as our emotions rather than a spreadsheet created the refurb plan!

I did agree a great purchase price, and in twelve years this property only had three tenants, the most recent had been there for seven years. Finally in 2021, we sold the property for £125,000 after a £8,000 full refurb. The profit of (£125,000-£75,000-£6,000) £44,000 before tax was an increase of just over 1.65% on the original purchase. Of course, there were years of rental profit as well. It is one of the most profitable deals we made, but through luck rather than expertise.

Overall conclusions:

- Be led by your spreadsheet but remain human rather than a shark.
- Make a logical plan and follow it.
- Know your area, your building type, your prospective client and above all the maths and money involved.

Full Time Job vs. Full Time Property Investor

By Latoya McDonald

I'm Latoya, also known as 'The Kiwi', and when I moved to the UK from New Zealand back in December 2010, I did not hang about when it came to taking action; I took a job on the high street within a corporate lettings and estate agency, and in 2012 I launched my Rent-to-Rent business and it really took off! Nothing was stopping me! I even did Rent-to-Rent on Guaranteed Rent properties - with the original Guaranteed Rent high street agent, who would've thought that would be possible? I did.

For those who don't know what Rent-to-Rent is, it is where you lease a property from an owner, providing them with guaranteed rent, and then you sub-let the property out. Normally, this is in the form of you renting a large property, say six bedrooms, and then you rent out each bedroom individually. You collect all the rent from your tenants in the 6 bedrooms, pay your rent to the owner, and whatever is left is for you to keep.

After several years, a landlord death, Rent-to-Rent property hand-backs, a Rent-to-Rent property sale (having to evict tenants due to those handbacks and sale), purchasing a few of our own HMOs, being offered properties that didn't meet my minimum profit so I took them on as managements. The Rent-to-Rent business started to take a turn and somewhere around the four-year mark, the business started to transition away from Rent-to-Rent.

From there, what I had was a fully functioning lettings and property management business, managing HMOs, single lets too, and working six days a week 'in' the business on; the team, the systems, legislation, with limited holidays - this was a nightmare!

How did I go from being an ambitious property investor with dreams of working 'on' my business, to working my arse off 'in' the business?

Some people might think having a large Rent-to-Rent business is a dream. Leaving the 'day job' and working within property full time, but if you're idea of a dream is being responsible for 20 large properties with 120-odd tenants along with hiring and training staff, managing legislation and fire safety, limited holidays and they've all got your mobile number, not to mention the furniture you collect and store, I can tell you those early days are a nightmare!

Don't get me wrong, I love my business, I have no children so this truly is my baby. I'm an HMO nutter and pride myself on being known for managing HMOs well. I've put in a lot of hard work, and I'm proud of my business and what myself and my team have achieved but, I do think this is something that is not taught on the Rent-to-Rent courses. What do you do when the Rent-to-Rent business changes? Yes, you adapt, but how?

Let's say you go from 20 Rent-to-Rents down to five over an eight-year period. The cost of running 20 Rent-to-Rents is greater than the costs of running five. For 20, perhaps you've got staff to pay for, van(s) to pay for, business costs to cover, but for five, could you do it yourself? But then if it's just you, how do you have a break? Go on holiday? Is the cost of having five Rent-to-Rents really worth it?

Now let's say, on top of the five Rent-to-Rents, you've bought five HMOs, you now have 10 HMOs, 60 tenants. Slightly too much for yourself to do and keep your lifestyle, but not enough to pay staff and yourself, what do you do?

This point is a conundrum that I think all large Rent-to-Rent businesses face.

Where I think the downfall of Rent-to-Rent is, if you don't achieve your goal within the set timeframe of the lease you've pretty much just have a job. There is nothing wrong with a job, but if I had a choice to work a 9-to-5 employed versus having 1-or-2 Rent-to-Rents self-employed, I'd choose the employed 9-to-5! At least I could still do 1-or-2 Rent-to-Rents whilst working and I'd have the benefit of more lenders available for when I want to buy too.

Now, within this 'story' I've not accounted for is working with investors to buy property and so on. I could go on-and-on about this and go into great details about options, business planning etc. but I think you get the gist of what I'm saying; when you create a large Rent-to-Rent business there comes a point where it might not be worth keeping the business anymore vs. transitioning to a managing agent to keep cash flow coming in (multiple streams of income and all that!).

What next for me and my business?

The lettings and property management business is well established, with a great team in place, so it's here to stay (and make the lives of HMO owners much easier!).

This leaves me with time to work 'on' my property acquisitions, which is the best position for me to be in. With hindsight, perhaps I would've done things differently. With so much knowledge about the Cornwall property market, perhaps I should've moved on from the Rent-to-Rent business and proceeded with working with investors on purchases. Interestingly, I'm doing that now and I have the added benefit of having my own letting agency to manage my properties exactly how I want them managed. So perhaps it's all worked out exactly as it should have? Perhaps this is the bit where I've woken up from the 'nightmare' to find it is all OK?

I hope this has been 'food for thought' within this niche and it gets those juices flowing about business planning and what you want your property investment career to look like.

Letting Agents Are Not Your Friends

By Vicki Wusche

Property is a business like any other. With a product or service and clients that demand perfection in return for their money. As a business all decisions need to be planned and logical, while as investors we are naturally greater risk takers that does not mean we need to take extreme risks.

It is also important to remember that you are a client and you need to see a return on your money and time invested and those that have invested in you. You need to be good at the maths and understand how the money flows – that's so obvious it should not need saying, but it does, because I regularly speak with people who have forgotten that one pivotal point.

When I work with clients, my goal is to save them time and money by leveraging my knowledge and experience. When I hand over a cash flowing investment, I explain all the processes to the client and place them with a trusted letting agent, part of my own team. A letting agent is a profit-making business in their own right. They charge a low fee for collecting rent and managing the tenants which can be time consuming. If you let them carry out repairs, they will add a fee, they need to as they need to cover their time.

You can have an excellent relationship with your letting agent, you can be friendly, but you still need to manage them as if they were an employee and you were their manager because they will drop the ball occasionally. Their staff team will change. My number one statement to my clients is that the letting agent is not a friend, they are in a sense an employee. They work for you and must offer a good service for a fair price.

One client, a very chatty lady, got too friendly with their letting agent, someone that I had recommended, let's call them Agency A in this story. In the beginning Agency A was on the ball. As with all good entrepreneurs, the owner was soon expanding their business and with that, they lost sight of their responsibility to ensure exceptional service to their existing landlords.

I had a number of clients with Agency A and so was able to see the problem before any individual landlord could. I advised all my clients to change agents. I sourced a new local partner and introduced everybody to Agency B.

Two of my clients had formed a deeper relationship with the lead contact, called Paris, in Agency A. They did not want to change letting agents, as I recommended, instead they followed Paris as she broke off and formed his own new one-woman band agency – this should always be a danger sign. Especially as Paris was in effect the lead staff member in the failing Agency A - how was she ever going to be successful on her own?

Now a year had past, most of my clients were happy in the new recommended relationship, enjoying full properties and punctual rent, from the proactive Agency B. One client who had moved with Paris formerly of Agency A, was experiencing voids, leaving them no alternative in their eyes, but to finally take over the management themselves.

My client still stayed, against advice, with Paris in her newly owned letting agents, even though every month the rent was incorrect. The rent was misallocated, late, or part paid. It got so bad that a tenant was found to be missing significant payments.

This is a perfect example of why you must take oversight of the rent even if you use a bookkeeper!

After a lot of encouragement, I persuaded my client to allow another of my team to gain entry to the property on the pretext of restructuring the investment strategy. The photos that came back were shocking. This new property looked like a dump, as if it had not been refurbed for 7-10 years rather than just two. I used another of my team – a letting agent from another area, to carry out an investigation of the accounts and to unpick what had been happening.

The summary is that as Paris's new letting agent business grew and she bought in new and inexperienced staff, combined with the distractions of her own business growth, proper systems simply fell by the wayside.

My client's tenants had been allocated to wrong rooms, with incorrect agreements, rent collections were missed, guarantors forgotten and inspections never carried out. The client lost £3,100 in rent and incurred a £5,096 refurb bill. I supported them to sue the agent for negligence and finally they followed advice and moved to the Agency B that I had recommended. Now their property is full and rent paid on time!

This was an expensive lesson in business management. It is worth remembering:

- You are one of many landlords that an agent has to deal with. A good relationship is not only beneficial, but necessary. Remember that an agent's responsibility is to manage your property and give good service, but it is also to run a profit-making business for themselves. You can be friendly, but they are not your friends.
- When they don't perform, call them out and if that does not change the service you are getting then find a new agent who can deliver the service you want and are prepared to pay for.
- Check everything, read the ASTs, get second quotes on repairs, inspect your own properties every three years. Know whether your tenants are employed, unemployed, families or single. This is your investment and your name is on the mortgage, the debt is yours alone to service and that requires rent to be paid, correctly on time, first time.
- Insist on regular photographic inspections, diary the dates so you don't forget. Insist on a guarantor, I have these even for working clients as they can lose a job and become unemployed as much as the next person. A deposit is never enough to cover rent and repairs when it is needed.

Property is like a business. The houses are not your home. You are providing a quality service for which you agree payment and other terms, such as care of the property.

You work with a team, one of which is your letting agent. You need to be their best customer, favourite customer even, and they must provide a quality and professional service. If not sack them and move on – it really is that simple.

Waking Up From the Nightmare

By Jackie Tomes

Extended timelines are costly when you are on bridging/development finance. Delays cost money, and all loans have agreed 'terms'. These deadlines loom heavily in the future when things are not going according to plan. The impact of this on your mental wellbeing can be big with stress and anxiety leading to bad night's sleep, poor eating and just generally struggling to focus.

What happens when multiples of these 'nightmares' happen at once? Imagine multiple elements outside of your control all hitting at once. No matter how hard you work or how creative you are, you have so little control over the overall outcome (or at least that's how it feels at the time). Imagine you weren't just having ongoing issues with utilities, and lack of power on site, but also at the same time issues with building control and the structural engineers! Imagine if the planners seem to be actively working against you at the same time as your finance company is. Or worse, imagine if the utilities, building control, structural engineers, planning and even finance company all seemed to join a club where they made a pact to make your project as difficult as possible to the point at which you felt as if you were wading through treacle because nothing and no one seemed to be on your side.

Do you feel your heart rate rising? Beads of sweat forming on your forehead? You are experiencing a weird mix of both hot and cold at the same time? Appetite gone? Exhausted, but at the same time feel like there's no way you could sleep at the sound of all those compounded nightmares?

I can confirm that is exactly what happens when all these things happen on the same project. Because they did. To me!

My previous stories are not from different projects. All of these stories are from one project: the project from hell. That was my real property nightmare!

It felt like everything that could have gone wrong, did go wrong, and these are just the 'highlights' of what went wrong, not an exhaustive list! Needless to say, it wasn't a profitable project, but I still own it. The cash flow is great and long term it is a great asset within the portfolio. It ended up being a university degree in commercial conversions. Whilst it was one of the most horrendous and stressful experiences of my life, I did learn a lot.

Here's the top five lessons this experience has taught me:

1. **Hire slowly, fire fast**

Do massive due diligence on all team and test on smaller projects first. Take time to choose the team and start doing it before there's a project ready to go so there's plenty of time. When someone starts not delivering on what they've promised or making errors, my rule is now once, twice; never again! Whilst it may seem worse to fire a member of the team and have the site sitting empty, it's not! They aren't the right person for the job and you'll be worse off in a few weeks/months' time if the tough decision isn't made now.

2. **Put in place a process that assumes everyone will let you down**

Follow-up processes are everything! When someone agrees to do something and by when, that date goes into our Task Management System, Asana, to follow-up at regular intervals to ensure it has been done, because otherwise there's a very high chance that it hasn't been!

3. **An expert power team who delivers, takes time to build**

The concept of a great 'power team' that you can hand over the keys to in order to deliver is great, but it takes time to build that team and until it's been expertly assembled you are going to have to be very involved.

4. Contingency isn't bonus money - you will spend it.

I used to look at that line 'contingency' on the deal analyser and think our deal analyser is so thorough we must have thought of everything and what could we possibly need those funds for. Safe to say I don't think that anymore! The more unknowns in the project or the less experience we have in that type of project the bigger that % contingency needs to be.

5. Commercial conversions are not for everyone

The big numbers on these projects look sexy! They can be alluring and it seems many of the property investment community aspire to ultimately be undertaking projects like these. I was one of them! This project taught me that I don't want to do projects like this. I'm a control freak and I also don't have much of an appetite for risk and that is OK. This project helped me to refine the deal criteria down to projects that require minimal involvement from other parties, so as much control as possible remains in my hands, therefore reducing the risk and maximising the sleep-well-at-night capabilities.

When I look back at the £2.8M GDV 17-unit conversion we almost did before this one, I cannot comprehend how out of our depth we would have been.

Looking back on it now, it was the best thing that I ever didn't do. I survived the 4-unit conversion, but I don't think it would have been the same on the 17-unit one!

So, this is me passing on the 'be careful' warning that I was so lucky to have received when we nearly 'jumped off a cliff' into the commercial conversion world. If you are considering moving into conversions or developments and you haven't built up the proper experience and team along the way, then please think carefully before you plunge in. The smaller projects along the way will have more than enough challenges to keep you interested!

Are you ready for more Property Nightmares?

Would you like to be featured in the next Property Nightmares?

Writing has begun on "Property Nightmares: Volume 2" and I am looking forward to publishing it in the future. If you would like to be kept up to date with more Property Nightmare books and the lessons learned, then please register your interest at www.propertynightmares.co.uk

Should you have any other feedback or comments, please contact me at hello@propertynightmares.co.uk or via social media.

I look forward to reading your reviews of the book.

Get in touch!

Angelos.

www.angelossanders.com

Printed in Great Britain
by Amazon

68021353R00197